painted
furniture

ROCKPORT

Dedication
For my parents.
—FH

For my father, who has been my inspiration.
—VP

First published in the United States of America by
Rockport Publishers, Inc.
33 Commercial Street
Gloucester, Massachusetts 01930-5089
Telephone: (978) 282-9590
Facsimile: (978) 283-2742
www.rockpub.com

ISBN: 1-56496-727-1

10 9 8 7 6 5 4 3 2 1

Design: Leeann Leftwich
Cover Image: Picture Press: Deco,
            Photographer: Nüttgens

Printed in China.

GLOUCESTER MASSACHUSETTS

ROCKPORT PUBLISHERS

painted
furniture

from simple scandinavian

to modern country

techniques by   text by

Virginia Patterson & Francine Hornberger

contents

BASICS OF
painting *furniture*

Painting is a great way to breathe new life into an old piece of furniture—or even to transform an ordinary newer piece of furniture into a focal point of a room. You may find an old end table in the attic or a piano bench at a yard sale. When you look at it, you're drawn to it, though you don't quite know why. You can see that even in a state of utter disrepair, the piece has an inherent charm. But how can you bring that out? This book provides several pattern and finish ideas that will inspire you to unlock the potential of any piece of furniture, from chairs to bureaus to tables to cabinets and more.

What you decide to paint is as important as how you decide to paint it. Obviously, a larger piece of furniture is going to make a stronger statement in a room than a smaller piece. Keep this in mind when you plan the piece. An elaborate and vibrant design painted on a large armoire is going to draw more attention than the same design on a small ladder-back chair. And conversely, a subtle stenciled pattern painted on a small, wall-mounted shelf may get lost, while the same pattern painted as a border treatment around the top of a dining room table will not.

As you begin, notice that each project is rated for level of difficulty:

a single paintbrush indicates no experience needed

two paintbrushes indicate easy projects

three paintbrushes indicate more challenging projects

four paintbrushes indicate projects to tackle once you have some experience

The Essentials

Before you begin any painted furniture project, make sure you are prepared. There's nothing worse than having to stop a project in the middle to run out and get the right size brush or the furniture wax you need to do an aging technique. Here are some basic materials that are always good to have on hand:

- Several sharpened number-two pencils
- White chalk
- Tracing paper
- Sheets of oak tag or thin cardboard
- Smudge-resistant carbon paper
- Screwdriver to remove furniture hardware
- Sandpaper ranging from extra-fine to medium grit
- Painter and artist brushes in various sizes
- Exacto knife and spare blades
- Ruler and/or T-square
- Drop cloths
- Several clean cotton rags
- Empty jars of various sizes—including film canisters—for storing portions of paint mixtures you've created plus containers such as coffee cans for mixing paint
- Stirring sticks for mixing colors
- Painter's masking tape of varying widths

BASICS OF
painting

Surfaces

More often than not, when you embark on a painted furniture project, you'll be working on wood. However, you may have an old metal cabinet that needs a facelift. Perhaps you bought a dresser in particleboard that you'd like to cheer up, or you'd rather paint over than replace the Formica in your kitchen. While it is possible to work with these surfaces—which we did in one example on page 47, the Seventies Chic cabinet—wood is by far the easiest surface to work with and is the surface we will be focusing on here.

Preparation

In this book, and especially in the patterns section, we focus on a particular section of the whole piece—a door, a drawer, a panel. But when you paint a piece of furniture, you have to deal with the piece as a whole.

Before you begin any painted furniture project, take a close look at the piece you will be painting. Are there any splits, knots, cracks, or missing chunks of wood that need to be filled? Also, if it is an old piece, is it stable?

Do any parts—like a chair leg—need to be replaced before you get started? You don't want to put in the painting time, only to have the piece fall apart on you when someone sits in it.

Does the piece have handles, knobs, pulls, or hinges? If so, remove these before getting started. It's easier to sand, clean, and paint the surface when hardware is already removed—even if you are planning to paint them in the same way as the piece. This will allow you to get a more even coverage on both the furniture and the hardware.

Does the piece have glass doors or partial glass doors? If so, remove them. Or, protect the glass from paint by masking off the perimeter of the glass with 1-inch (3 cm) masking tape. While you can always scrape off any paint you get on the glass with a razor blade later, peeling off masking tape is an easier, more time-effective method. Once you've addressed these issues, you can begin the process of getting your piece ready to paint.

furniture

When the piece is ready, place it on a drop cloth. You can use the plastic type available in any hardware store, or try an old sheet—at least for the sanding phase. When you're done with sanding, you'll be grateful to wrap the residue up and throw it away—and not break out the vacuum. Whatever material you are working with, the sanding phase is an integral part of the process. For all types of wood, you'll want to use a medium to fine-grit sandpaper—150 grit is best—to get the piece smooth and ready for painting. Too coarse a grit will score the surface, while too fine a grit will not achieve the required smoothness. You can sand the piece by hand, or use an electric sander, which will save a lot of time.

After you've completely sanded the piece, run your hand along it, looking for bumps and splinters. When you're satisfied with the smoothness of the surface, wipe away residue with a damp cloth or a tack cloth. Once this phase is completed, remove the drop cloth you used for sanding and replace it with a clean one for painting. While some projects don't require a piece to be primed before you begin painting, most will benefit from at least one coat of primer. For the projects in this book,

we used a water-based primer. A water-based primer is not only easier to clean from brushes, it also dries faster. Paint the entire piece of furniture with primer and allow each coat of primer to dry for at least two hours. Once the primer is dry, proceed with the base coat. Then follow the directions for the project you have chosen.

Brushes

You should have a variety of brushes of different sizes, thicknesses, shapes, and materials on hand before beginning a painted furniture project.

Sponge brushes are great for high-coverage projects—for painting primer and base coats. Depending on what you are painting, a 2- to 3-inch (5 to 8 cm) sponge brush will probably do the trick. The best part about sponge brushes is that they are inexpensive and disposable—no clean-up needed. Also, for projects that require a very smooth surface, such as the Mediterranean Lacquer piece on page 97, you don't have to worry about bristle marks—or stray bristles. They create smooth, even strokes.

Wide-bristle brushes (2- to 3-inch [5 to 8 cm]) are also good for large coverage projects, like painting the primer and base coats. The coverage you get from a bristle brush is basically the same as with sponge brush, but less smooth. Rule of thumb: quality counts when using these types of brushes. When properly cleaned, you can hold on to a high-quality brush forever. A low-quality brush will fall apart after a few uses.

Smaller sponge or bristle brushes (1-inch [3 cm]) are great for touch ups. It's always good to have a few of these on hand. Art brushes are essential for detail work, intricate patterns, and small areas. These come in all different sizes, shapes, and densities. Round brushes are best for filling in templates, while flat brushes work great for painting areas between masking tape. Use a liner brush for thin borders, outlines, and details.

Paint

For most of the projects in this book, we either used latex-based household interior paint or acrylic art paint.

The household interior paint works perfectly for base coats, finishes, and many of the patterns. Unless the project calls for you to use a flat, satin, or high-gloss paint, the finish you use can be determined by your own personal preference. The best thing about using household paint is that you can have colors mixed for you right in the store. Also, it is easier to work with than acrylic paint, going on smoother and more evenly and requiring less maintenance.

Acrylic paint should be reserved for small applications, such as the decorative elements of a design, as opposed to the basecoat, which should be applied using latex paint. Please note that when using acrylics, you will probably have to mix it with a little water, due to the thickness of the paint. You'll want your basecoat to be thinner (with the consistency of ordinary latex interior paint), while paint for smaller patterns—like the polka dots in the Polka-Dot Whimsy project on page 30 and the stars in its variation—can be worked without watering down the paint at all.

One of the projects in the book calls for spray paint. Spray paints are ideal for covering large, metal furniture pieces, however, we recommend only using spray paints in temperate climates. While spray paint provides for very even and fast coverage, it must be applied outdoors. In cold weather, spray paint has a tendency to crack. If you do use spray paint, follow manufacturer's directions carefully and heed all temperature recommendations.

Don't underestimate the need for a finishing coat on any project. Without it, your piece will not be able to stand any wear and tear without chipping or scratching. In most of the projects featured, we use a clear polyurethane spray. The finish selected, whether high gloss, semigloss, stain, or flat, is determined by the individual project. In addition to providing protection to the furniture surface, the finishing coat also makes the colors more vibrant.

In the Mix

How can you get the colors you want if you can't readily find them? Here are some simple formulas for colors we used in this book:

- **Coral pink:** mix 1 part white with ¼ part red
- **Hot pink:** mix 1 part white with ½ part red
- **Peach:** mix 2 parts white with ¼ part red and ¼ part yellow
- **Bright orange:** mix 1 part yellow with ¼ part red
- **Bright yellow:** mix ¼ part white with 1 part yellow
- **Light green:** mix 3 parts white with 1 part green
- **Olive green:** mix 1 part green with 1 part yellow, ⅓ part red, and 2 parts white
- **Aquamarine:** mix 1 part cobalt blue with ¼ part red
- **Periwinkle:** mix 2 parts white with 1 part blue, ¼ part red
- **Light blue:** mix 1 part blue with 6 parts white
- **Sky blue:** 1 part white with ¼ part blue
- **Medium blue:** mix 1 part blue with 3 parts white
- **Bright green:** mix 1 part green with ¼ part yellow and ¼ part white
- **Lavender:** mix 1 part white with ½ part blue and ¼ part red

right for *the room*

When you paint a piece of furniture, there are many more elements to consider than just the "how to." A piece of painted furniture can have as much impact in a space as the color of the walls, the material used on the floors, or the window treatments. It can become the focal point of a room, changing the mood of a décor or even setting the tone for the rest of the interior design scheme to follow.

With that in mind, how to paint any particular piece of furniture should not be a decision you make lightly. Before you begin, step back and take a good look at the room where the piece will be housed. What is the room already conveying? Are there architectural elements to emphasize? How will the painted piece contrast with or complement other furnishings in the room? If the room doesn't already have a personality of its own, how can you give it one with the addition of a painted piece?

Taking inspiration from the existing décor is one way to decide what kind of project to undertake, but it's not the only way. Flip through interior design magazines and books. Do you have a favorite style that you always seem to stop on but are afraid to change your whole room with this look? Perhaps you've fallen in love with French country style, but you live in a contemporary home or a modern high-rise apartment building and you think that bringing that style in simply won't work against that background. Instead, satisfy your taste for French country style by distressing a small bench in your living room, or using an aging technique on a bureau. On the other hand, if you live in a nineteenth-century farmhouse, and you want to go full force on French country style, distressing the built-in cabinets in your family room or other prominent aspect of your home might just be the best way to start revamping your décor.

Think of how a small, round, bent-leg end table painted with a simple, English floral motif can infuse an entryway with charm. At one time an unnoticed drop point for keys and mail, the table now becomes a welcoming beacon into a tastefully decorated home. Consider how an old wooden chair, at one time an afterthought employed to fill an empty corner in the living room, can become a place where the guest of honor sits when painted in a rich, black lacquer with a gold-leaf motif. Imagine how a vibrantly painted striped shelf can brighten up an otherwise ordinary powder room—and still provide much-needed storage.

And isn't that what really sets a piece of painted furniture apart from other decorative aspects in a room, like wallpaper or art? By its very nature, furniture is for function. A chair is for sitting on. An armoire is for hiding clothes, and an entertainment center disguises a home office. A table is for dining, working, or gathering. But with a decorative paint treatment or a fresh coat of paint, these pieces become the art itself, elements that infuse a room with visual interest and that can ultimately become the focal point of any room.

PAIRING
pattern & style

Choosing patterns to enhance your décor is, at heart, a personal process. While you may choose a pattern because you think it will set a particular style or mood in a room, if you don't intrinsically like the pattern, you're not going to be happy with the result. It may sound obvious, but if you are tempted to create a distinctively English country bedroom, and florals don't really do it for you, you'll be treading on dangerous ground if you include too many floral patterns in your design scheme. Do the research. Find out everything you can about a style and what goes into making that style before you get carried away with implementing it. When you learn more about English country style, you see that it's a rich style that relies on many different patterns—and in many cases, these patterns are all used together. So instead of florals, you might opt for a scheme that relies on plaids to get the point across, with small floral touches—perhaps in the form of a couple of tiny throw pillows for the bed, that are subtle enough to blend in with the décor but that are easily removed when you want a different look.

PAIRING
pattern & style

The same holds true for painting furniture. A distinctive piece can, in and of itself, set the décor for an entire room, so painting a piece of furniture with a particular pattern—especially if it is a large piece and an intricate pattern—will affect the mood of the space. Think about the piece in relation to the other elements of the room. If the walls of your dining room are covered from floor to ceiling in a lively print, an equally lively painted sideboard will more than likely only compete with that piece and lead to an environment with too much going on—not the ideal for a space where the concentration needs to be placed on the food and the company. However, if the only pattern in the room exists in a wallpaper border, consider picking up this border pattern on the sideboard—an effect that will not only liven up the space but also tie it together.

But not all painted furniture needs to be part of a planned and defined scheme to be an integral part of the design. Perhaps you've always been a fan of paisley or polka dots. While these patterns can be conformed to a specific style, through size of the patterns and color choices, they are great stand-alones. Imagine a lavender plant table with a paisley border (see page 72) adding a touch of whimsy to a muted beige sunroom or a painted-white baker's rack adorned in large, bright red polka dots making a playful statement in an otherwise stark and serious kitchen.

The projects in this book will inspire designs and combinations for every style. Remember, the proof is often in the combinations, so keep in mind these classics as you plan.

- Small floral prints in muted shades are a romantic favorite.

- Big blocks of hot colors make a strong statement in a casual contemporary home.

- A simple motif in the light hand of Swedish style provides a relaxed country look.

PAIRING
finish & style

If pattern does not suit your taste, the right finish can be just what is needed to make your piece stand out in—or even establish—your décor. Like pattern, how you decide on a finish should first be dictated by aesthetic preference, not what you think you should do. For example, you might have a real penchant for country décor, but that doesn't mean it should translate to your furniture—especially if the thought of peeling paint makes you want to want to break out the sandpaper and make repairs. Gingham curtains may be just what you need to curb your country craving. And while you may admire the look of a high-gloss lacquer seen in a friend's home, it might not be the best match on an everyday basis for your own home.

To decide on a finish and technique, think about what look you wish to incorporate in your space. Highbrow and elegant? Timeworn and casual? Sleek and modern? There's a finish for every look. And remember, as with patterns, you can juxtapose a finished piece into a décor where you think it might not belong to surprising effect. Consider the statement a wardrobe painted in masculine colors like hunter green, burgundy, and navy blue can make in a delicate all-white bedroom decorated with gauzy curtains and an Art Nouveau–style iron bed. Or how a simple colorwashed chair can soften a stark modern décor.

For the design purist, however, keeping within the parameters of a particular style is the only way to go. In those cases, choose paint finishes for furnishings that complement and emphasize the look and mood you are trying to convey. A foyer table painted in a faux marble finish that perhaps picks up the pattern of the marble floor below says to the guest that he has just entered an elegant home, where every detail has been carefully considered. Now

imagine the same entryway—this time with a floor of rough-hewn slate. And in place of the faux marble table, visualize a Shaker bench treated with a pickled finish. Furniture in and of itself can affect décor, but furniture painted in a decorative finish takes it one step further and seals the deal.

If you want to create a feeling of country casual in your home, try techniques such as distressing (page 89), crackling (page 108), and aging (page 91). These techniques make furniture pieces look as though they've been around for generations—and have become beloved family members. But country encompasses more than timeworn finishes. To capture the charm of Shaker, Amish, and rustic looks, use milk paints or thinned-out latex to replicate the worn, transparent look of antique finishes. Pickling (page 105) and Shaker rub (page 84) are great finish alternatives that don't involve peeling paint.

Looking for something sleek and contemporary? A lacquer treatment (page 97) on a wooden table or chair imbues a room with modern elegance. Or, try moving beyond wood. With a high-gloss spray paint, transform a standard-issue metal cabinet into a colorful focal point. Or, try out paints that mimic the look of stone, such as granite paint.

Whatever you decide, be sure not to practice your technique on the piece itself. Take some trial runs until you really feel comfortable with a particular treatment. And if you really love it, why not continue it on the walls or floor? In that way, your painted furniture piece becomes not only an element in a design scheme but actually establishes the mood of the room.

painted *patterns*

This Beach Cabana Bureau is perfect for a seaside cottage—or even for an urban space decorated to suggest a home by the sea. In this relatively easy project, only the drawer fronts are painted. The natural exposed pine calls to mind the boardwalk at the beach, while the playful colorful stripes echo umbrellas, beach balls, and care-free summer days.

beach cabana *bureau*

TIP

When working with pine, you may have to contend with knots. Generally, the primer will cover these. For really stubborn knots, apply wood filler to the knot and sand carefully before applying the primer.

Method

- Study the photo on the facing page. Simply by careful measuring, masking, and painting you can transform a plain pine dresser into this perky cabana-style piece. Before you start, practice on scrap pieces of plywood or like surface.

- Be sure to cut each piece of masking tape long enough so that it overhangs each side. This will make it easier to pull off.

- Take care that the masking tape is straight and free of air bubbles on the drawer fronts. While a slightly imperfect line will give the piece charm, rough, jagged or blurred lines just look messy.

- Do not paint completely over the tape, as this will make the tape more difficult to remove.

- Also note that you will need ten to twelve hours to complete the project. Perform steps 1 through 3 on all drawer fronts before proceeding. Steps 4 through 6 should be completed within four hours to avoid problems removing the masking tape.

PAINTING SURFACE
A three-drawer dresser in unfinished pine (other light woods will work just as well)

PATTERN
None required

COMPLETION TIME
Twelve hours (including drying time)

RATING ✒

starting *out*

Step 1 Remove drawers from dresser. Unscrew knobs from drawers and put aside. Sand down the drawer fronts one at a time. Wipe with tack cloth to remove residue. Apply primer to each drawer front. Using the widest brush, paint with the grain of the wood. Allow first coat to dry for at least two hours. Paint over the primer coat with the bright white base coat, painting with the grain.

Step 2 Line up the ruler on the left side of the drawer front, working with one drawer at a time. With pencil, mark 7/8-inch (2 cm) increments. Using the T-square, draw light pencil lines across the drawer fronts at these increments.

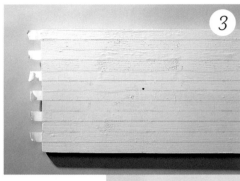

Step 3 Line up strips of masking tape just above the bottom of every other line. Make sure the masking tape strips extend about an inch beyond each side of the drawer. This will make it easier to pull them off. Important: manufacturers recommend removing the tape within four hours, so apply only to drawers you will be painting right away. Do not place masking tape until basecoat is completely dry.

Step 4 Select a paint color for the first drawer. With a 5/8-inch (1.5 cm) flat art brush, paint lightly and evenly over the exposed sections of the drawer front. Do not paint completely over the tape or it will be sealed to the drawer. A heavy coat of paint will make the tape brittle and difficult to peel and might cause the color to bleed under the tape, ruining the striped effect. Apply two coats of paint, allowing each to dry for at least forty-five minutes.

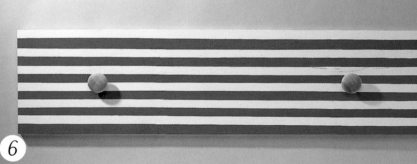

Step 5 Gently peel off the masking tape, row by row. Important: manufacturers recommend removing the tape within four hours, so for best results, remove masking tape as soon as the second color coat dries. Touch up uneven areas with a 5/16-inch (8 mm) flat art brush. Repeat steps 4 through 6 with remaining drawer fronts.

Step 6 Apply polyurethane finish. Two coats are recommended. When drawer front is completely dry, reattach drawer pulls.

v a r i a t i o n

For a more complicated variation, try wider or even vertical stripes. Or, paint waves on the drawers instead of straightforward stripes. Check craft and notions stores for beach-themed stencils or decals, and instead of taking the stripes the whole way across on one drawer, paint a seashell on that end.

Method

Create irregular stripes in soft colors with a subtractive method of decorative painting. Prepare drawer fronts as in steps 1 and 2 using icy blue instead of bright white for the basecoat. Apply a thin coat of accent color and remove by wiping the wet paint with the cardboard strips to create a striped pattern revealing the base coat below.

TIP

Make sure your accent color is not thinned so much that it runs, and work quickly so that it does not set before you use the cardboard strips. If you make a mistake, you can wipe it off with a clean rag and start again.

Materials

- Two cardboard strips, 1 3/4 inches (4 cm) wide and 5/8 inch (1.5 cm) wide.
- Base coat color, icy blue latex semigloss
- Accent color, citrus yellow latex semigloss

- Fine sandpaper
- Tack cloth to remove dust
- Three paintbrushes: one 2-inch (5 cm) wide for primer and base coat; one ¼" (6 mm) round artist's brush for painting polka dots; and one ¹⁄₁₆" (1.5 mm) round artist's brush for touch-ups
- One small can of latex-based primer
- A number-two pencil
- One small container of acrylic paint, in olive green*
- One small can container of acrylic paint, in peach*
- One small can container of acrylic paint, in periwinkle*
- One spray can satin-finish polyurethane

Note: You will need a larger container of paint in the color you choose to paint the rest of the piece.

PAINTING SURFACE
An unfinished pine bureau

PATTERN
A quarter or other coin in the size of your choice

COMPLETION TIME
Ten hours
(including drying time)

RATING

Make an ordinary dresser the focal piece of a room—it just takes a bit of color and a simple pattern. This dresser, with its brightly colored drawer fronts and playful polka dots, could easily be at home in a kid's room or in the master bedroom.

polka-dot *whimsy*

TIP

Instead of tracing the coin over and over on the drawer front, trace it many times on a piece of cardboard. Cut out the coin shapes, and lay them over the drawer front in the pattern shown on page 31, or in one of your choosing. This will provide a complete visual before the dresser gets marked up. Trace the dots onto the drawer front and proceed with the project as follows.

Method

- Before you begin, study the photo on the opposite page. This project requires sanding, priming, and painting with a pattern you can easily master. Experiment with your technique on a piece of scrap wood before you get to the actual piece.

- You don't have to use a quarter. For bigger polka dots, you can try a silver dollar; for smaller ones, a nickel or a penny might make your best choice.

- Take your time and paint in the polka dots with care. While you can touch-up either color once you've finished, it's better—and easier—to get it right the first time.

starting *out*

Remove drawers from dresser. Unscrew knobs from drawers and put aside. Sand down the drawer fronts one at a time and then sand down dresser. Wipe with a tack cloth to remove residue. Apply primer to each drawer front with the 2 inch (5 cm) brush. Paint with the grain of the wood. Allow first coat to dry, and, if needed, apply a second coat and allow to dry for an additional two hours.

Step 1 Following the grain of the wood, paint over the primer coat on one of the drawer fronts with the olive green base coat, using the 2-inch (5 cm) brush. Let dry. Apply a second coat and let dry.

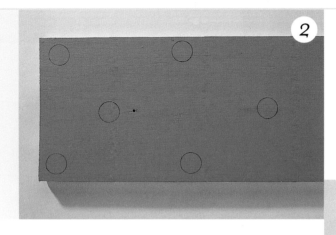

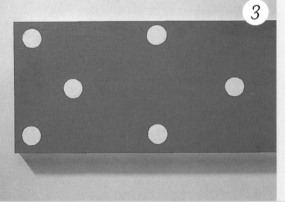

Step 2 Arrange coins or cardboard cutouts on drawer front, playing around with position until you find the most appealing arrangement, or follow the arrangement provided in the photo on page 29. With pencil, trace the polka-dot templates, pressing firmly so you can clearly see the outlines.

Step 3 Taking the ¼" (6 mm) round paintbrush, fill in the polka dots with the peach paint. Touch-up uneven areas with a ¹⁄₁₆" (1.5 mm) round artist's brush. Repeat steps 1 through 3 with remaining drawer fronts, using the periwinkle as a base coat for one and the peach as a base coat for the other. Here, the olive green-colored drawer has peach polka dots, but you can use the blue if you choose. Just limit your color choices to a total of three to give the piece a sense of unity.

TIP

Experiment with different ways to apply paint. Instead of using the traditional bristle or sponge brush, try ragging on paint or applying with a sea sponge for a completely different effect.

4

Step 4 Apply polyurethane finish to drawer fronts. Two coats are recommended. When drawer fronts are completely dry, reattach knobs. Apply a coat of primer to the dresser frame. Allow to dry for two hours, and apply a second coat, which should dry for an additional two hours. Paint the remainder of the dresser in olive, peach, or periwinkle, and be sure to paint two coats all around. We chose olive, but your décor may call for one of the other colors to be emphasized. Apply two coats of polyurethane finish, and allow the piece to dry overnight.

whimsy variation

Not a fan of polka dots? Create star, moon, heart, shell, or whatever–shape–you–like templates. Check craft and notions stores for stencils or decals. For larger shapes, try cookie cutters. Find whimsical knobs and drawer pulls in housewares stores to complete your theme. This is a simple variation that sets the theme of bright stars on a night sky.

Method

Follow the directions for Polka-Dot Whimsy on pages 30–32, this time substituting new colors and the star templates for the polka dots. Trace star template on page 115 onto tracing paper. Carefully cut out template drawn on tracing paper and trace onto oak tag. Create several templates—so you can lay them out across your drawer—and carefully cut out. Proceed as directed.

TIP

Get inspiration from the other design elements in the room where you plan to put the dresser. Is there any one element that could be tied into the dresser? How about the finials on the curtain rods or an interesting shade pull? Is there a wallpaper border with a simple shape you could pick up and echo on the dresser?

Materials

Have the same materials on hand for the variation, but include the following:

- A sheet of tracing paper to trace star template
- A number-two pencil
- One sheet of oak tag or thin, clean cardboard
- One small container of acrylic paint, in aquamarine
- One small container of acrylic paint, in bright yellow
- Small containers of acrylic paint for the other colors you'll introduce for the other drawers and the dresser itself

Life's a party, so add a little fiesta to your kitchen, living room, even bedroom. This vibrantly patterned project is a perfect complement to an already colorful room (as shown) but can also be a welcome splash of color in an otherwise plain décor. The bright colors aren't typical of southwestern style, but the patterns make an undeniable southwestern statement.

southwestern *fiesta*

TIP

You can use a T-square to line up the placement of your stripes, but you may find that a 12-inch or 18-inch (30 cm or 46 cm) ruler is more manageable.

Method

- This piece is all about pattern and color. With its carefully drawn templates, a little masking tape, and a rainbow of colors, it's challenging and time consuming—but well worth the effort. This project demonstrates the pattern on the lower section of the cabinet doors. Pattern templates for this section, as well as the top sections, are available on pages 116–117.

- Practice drawing and coloring in these templates on oak tag or ideally, on scrap pieces of wood before you work on the cabinet. The colors in this cabinet are very rich and vibrant, and the fewer mistakes you make, the less tedious the touch-up work.

- If you are working on a cabinet, remove the doors. The pattern will be much easier to execute flat.

- Always work on the patterned sections before painting the unpatterned sections of your piece. You can always work on these sections while your patterned pieces are drying between steps.

Materials

- Screwdriver to match cabinet-hardware screws
- Fine sandpaper
- Tack cloth to remove dust
- One small can of latex-based primer
- One 2-inch (5 cm) brush; one 1/2-inch (1 cm) flat art brush; one 1/4-inch (6 mm) flat art brush
- One small can of water-based primer
- T-square (optional)
- 12- or 18-inch (30 cm or 46 cm) ruler
- One roll of 1-inch-wide (3 cm) painter's masking tape
- One small container of acrylic paint, in cadmium red (ready-made)
- One small container of acrylic paint, in cobalt blue (ready-made)
- One small container of acrylic paint, in sky blue
- One small container of acrylic paint, in bright green
- One small container of acrylic paint, in bright orange
- One small container of acrylic paint, in cadmium yellow, medium (ready-made)
- One spray can satin-finish polyurethane

PAINTING SURFACE
An unfinished pine cabinet

PATTERN
A series of templates (found on pages 116–118)

COMPLETION TIME
Twenty-four hours (including drying time)

RATING ////

starting *out*

Trace and cut out templates on pages 116–118 and set aside. Remove doors from cabinet. Unscrew any knobs or hardware and put them aside. Sand down the cabinet doors one at a time. Sand the remainder of the cabinet. Wipe with a tack cloth to remove residue. With the 2-inch (5 cm) brush, apply primer to each cabinet door, back side first, and allow to dry. Paint with the grain of the wood. Allow first coat to dry for at least two hours. If needed, apply a second coat and allow to dry for an additional two hours.

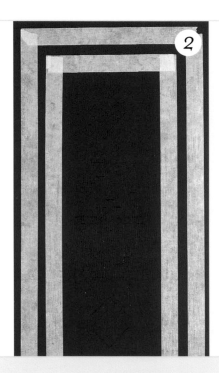

Step 1 With 2-inch (5 cm) brush, paint the back side of the cabinet door in the bright red paint, and allow to dry for at least an hour. Once dry, lay the backside down on a clean old sheet and proceed to paint the front sides in bright red, with the grain. Allow first coat to dry for at least two hours, and paint a second coat of bright red. Allow base coat to dry overnight.

Step 2 With a ruler or T-square, measure the width of the cabinet doors, measuring in from the outside edges of the cabinet doors. Precisely where you decide to put your stripes will depend on the width of your doors. (We measured in 4 inches [10 cm].) Mark these points with a number-two pencil. Take your T-square or ruler and lightly draw in lines to mark the position of your masking tape. Line the masking tape up along the inner perimeter of your pencil lines, making a rectangle. With your ruler, measure out from this inside rectangle about 1 inch (3 cm). Mark these points with the number-two pencil, then with your ruler or T-square, draw lines to mark the position of your outer masking tape rectangle.

Step 3 Once you've established the position of your border, experiment with the placement of your templates. You can use a ruler to designate equal distances for top and bottom and right and left placement. Once you have your templates in place, trace them onto the board with the number-two pencil. With the ½-inch (1 cm) flat art brush, paint the border in cobalt blue, trying not to paint too much over the masking tape itself, as this will make the tape difficult to remove. Allow to dry for about twenty minutes then, paint a second coat.

(Note: If you are using acrylic paint, do not thin the blue paint.)

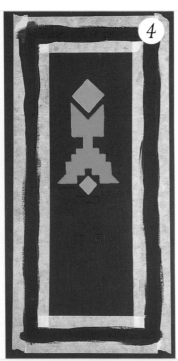

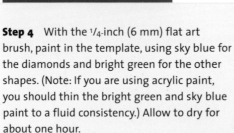

Step 4 With the ¼-inch (6 mm) flat art brush, paint in the template, using sky blue for the diamonds and bright green for the other shapes. (Note: If you are using acrylic paint, you should thin the bright green and sky blue paint to a fluid consistency.) Allow to dry for about one hour.

Step 5 Carefully remove the masking tape. Touch-up the door as necessary. Apply polyurethane finish to front and back of cabinet doors. Two coats are recommended. Using the picture on page 34 as your guide, repeat these steps for the remaining cabinet doors. See pages 117–118 for remaining templates.

fiesta variation

For a more traditional southwestern feel, use the same patterns, but substitute pastel colors for the bold red and blue used in the original piece. Depending on the shape of your cabinet, you can use this pattern layout on the horizontal, or get really creative and vary the order and direction of the patterns.

Method

This variation is performed in the same way as the original project, using different colors. Because it may be difficult to see pencil over the dark purple basecoat, try tracing the template with white chalk. You can easily see it and whatever you don't paint over will simply wipe away once the piece is dry.

TIP

Keep in mind, you don't have to use these colors if others are more appealing to you. If you do choose other colors, please be sure to consult color directories, however, to make sure the ones you have selected will work well together. As an added precaution, you can actually paint the color scheme together on a piece of scrap wood before you begin.

Materials

Have the same materials on hand for the variation, but include the following:
• One small container of acrylic paint, in lavender
• One small container of acrylic paint, in coral pink

- Fine sandpaper
- Tack cloth
- Ruler
- Number-two pencil
- Chalk (optional)
- Masking tape
- Three paintbrushes: one 2-inch (5 cm) sponge brush for applying primer and base coat; one 1/4-inch (6 mm) round art brush for leaves; one 1/8-inch (3 mm) round liner brush for painting in vine and touch-ups
- One small can of water-based primer
- One small can of water-based, flat paint in pale sage green for basecoat
- One small can of water-based, flat paint in jasper green for vine
- One spray can satin-finish polyurethane

PAINTING SURFACE
An unfinished pine dresser

PATTERN
None required

COMPLETION TIME
**Four hours
(including drying time)**

RATING

Swedish colors are light and pastel, and that's the secret to creating the ultimate

Swedish piece. In this project, we transformed a plain wooden table into a vanity

by adding a simple apron to three sides. The piece is then finished with a pale mint–

green color creates a delightful backdrop for a simple vine pattern.

swedish *lights*

Method

- This simple vine pattern requires only a few careful brush-strokes, but it's a good idea to practice your technique a few times before painting the finished piece.

- Try to paint the vine freehand, or mark a pattern lightly in pencil or chalk to follow.

- For a more elaborate effect, paint the vine motif on, or around, the table's legs.

starting out

Sand the table and remove any residue with tack cloth or slightly damp cloth. With the 2-inch (5 cm) brush, apply the first coat of primer. Allow top to dry thoroughly and apply the second coat.

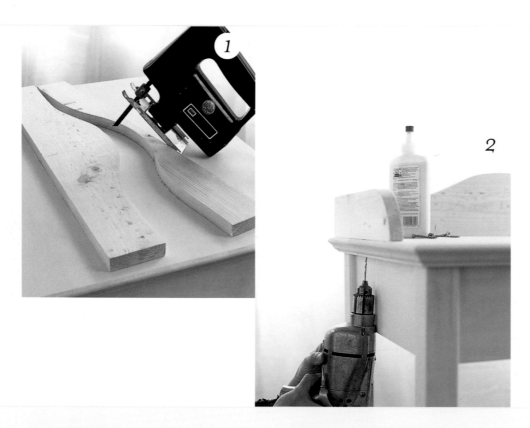

Step 1 Use a jigsaw to cut a wooden apron to fit around the back outside edge of the table. If you don't want to do this yourself, you may be able to have the wood cut for you at a home improvement store. Just bring a template.

Step 2 Secure the apron in place with strong wood glue. Drill through both layers to create a starter hole, then attach the apron firmly with wood screws.

With the 2-inch (5 cm) brush, apply two coats of primer to the table, allowing coats to dry thoroughly in between. With the 2-inch (5 cm) brush, paint the table completely in the light sage green base coat. Let dry thoroughly and apply a second coat.

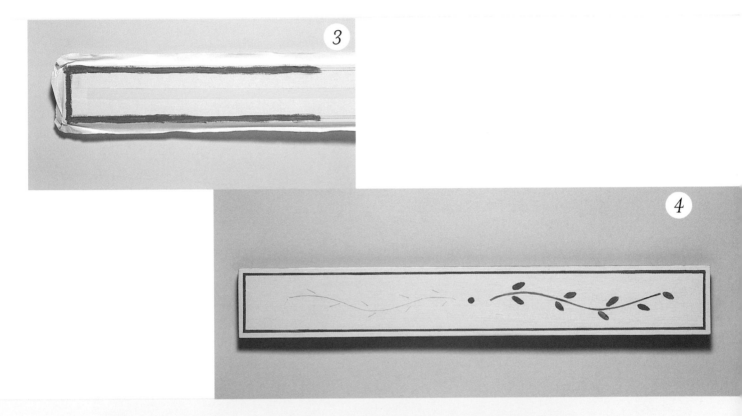

Step 3 With a ruler, measure in ½ inch (1 cm) from the edges of the front of table and mark with pencil or chalk. Mask off and paint border in jasper green with the ¼ inch (1 cm) round artist's brush. Carefully remove masking tape upon completion. Allow paint to dry thoroughly before moving to the next step.

Step 4 If you are more comfortable doing so, draw in the vine pattern lightly in pencil or in chalk. With the 1/8-inch (6 mm) round liner brush, paint in vine pattern, following the photo on page 41.

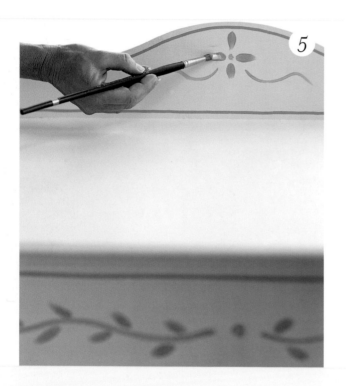

5

Step 5 Create a central floral motif as a centerpiece to two vines by painting four leaf shapes around a center dot. When the table is completely dry, spray with polyurethane top coat and let dry thoroughly.

TIP

Flat-finish paint gives a soft effect perfect for Swedish design as well as Colonial-style rooms and the like. The main problem with flat-finish paint, however, is that it is difficult to clean and should only be used on items that don't get a lot of wear and tear. An alternative for a piece in a high-volume area is eggshell finish. It is barely reflective, so you can keep a subdued appearance, but is much easier to clean.

variation

This variation mimics the original pattern, except that the pattern is more detailed and controlled. The antique white backdrop sets a delicate feel, perfect for a woman's vanity or dressing table. For a country look, change the colors. Try painting a blue leaf pattern over a beige background.

Method

This variation is performed in much the same way as the preceding project, but in this case, a tiny leaf shape was created, cut out, and traced around the vine, making for a more precise effect. First prime the table. Then paint two coats of the antique white basecoat. Once the basecoat has dried, create the border. Next, lightly draw in the vine with pencil or white chalk. Next, trace leaf shapes around the vine, following photo. Paint in vine using liner brush and leaves with round art brush.

Materials

- Fine sandpaper
- Tack cloth
- Ruler
- Number-two pencil
- Chalk (optional)
- Masking tape
- Three paint brushes: one 2-inch (5 cm) sponge brush for applying primer and base coat; one 1/4-inch (6 mm) round art brush for leaves; one 1/8-inch (3 mm) round liner brush for painting in vine and touch-ups
- One small can of water-based primer
- One small can of water-based, flat paint in antique white for basecoat
- One small can of water-based, flat paint in jasper green for vine
- One spray can satin-finish polyurethane

Bring a mod, retro feel into a living space with this cabinet, which features bold, brash, and bright colors and cool circle shapes. This cabinet is different than other projects in this book as it is done with spray paint on metal. Using a high-gloss spray paint ensures a true-to-life metallic finish.

Materials

- Fine-grit sandpaper
- Several large sheets of oak tag or lightweight cardboard
- Compass (optional)
- One can of water-based spray primer
- One can of spray paint, in apple red gloss
- Low-tack double-sided tape
- A roll of painter's masking tape
- One can of spray paint, in orange gloss
- One can of spray paint, in orange-yellow gloss
- One can of spray paint, in magenta gloss
- One spray can gloss-finish polyurethane

retro chic cabinet

TIP

When using spray paint, always work in a well-ventilated area. The best bet is to work outside, if possible. If working outside, make sure it's a still day. Any wind can cause particles to stick to wet paint. Keep in mind, however, that spray paint will crackle and peel in temperatures below 50°F.

Method

- For the best effect, create circles in different sizes. You can do this using the templates on page 120 or by using a compass to determine the sizes you want. Large circles are best for this project.

- Make sure the surface is completely smooth and free of any dust or dirt before painting.

- Allow coats of paint to dry thoroughly before moving on to the next step.

- Ensure that stencils are securely applied to the surface and that there are no gaps or tears in the stencil before painting so that paint will not get outside the circles. For best results, apply the low-tack double-sided tape to the inner edge of the circle to prevent paint from seeping under the stencil. Use masking tape as a secondary way to secure the stencil and to keep it from blowing around during spraying.

PAINTING SURFACE
A metal cabinet

PATTERN
A series of stencils (found on pages 120–121)

COMPLETION TIME
Thirty hours (including drying time)

RATING ////

starting *out*

Lightly sand the cabinet's surface to dull down the slick original finish. This allows the paint to adhere to the metal surface better, since paint easily peals from a slick surface. After sanding, clean with a slightly damp cloth. Spray with two light coats of primer. Trace stencils from page 120 onto oak tag or lightweight cardboard and cut out circle shapes. Set aside.

TIP

To bring out the inherent shininess of metal, it's a good idea to paint it with a high-gloss finish. The drawback of this type of finish, however, is that it will show every flaw, no matter how carefully you sand. Try painting in a semi-gloss finish and use a high-gloss topcoat.

1

Step 1 After letting the primer dry, spray on the red base coat. Let dry thoroughly and apply a second coat.

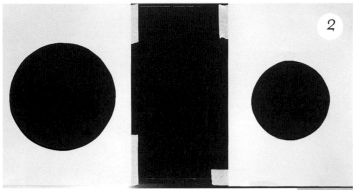

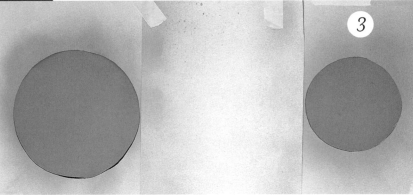

Step 2 Position stencils on the cabinet and secure the inner edges with low-tack double-sided tape and the outer edges with masking tape.

Step 3 Spray additional colors.

Step 4   To do corners or edges, bend stencils over side of cabinet and tape in place. Spray over the template. Spray the cabinet with gloss polyurethane top coat and let dry.

cabinet
variation

This variation features new shapes (templates on page 121) and bright colors: blue and yellow.

Method

Follow the directions on pages 48 to 50 to create this variation. Be sure to create stencils of all different sizes for a funky effect. These shapes will be trickier to work with than the standard circle stencil, so be sure to give yourself ample practice time—especially for shapes that drape over the top and sides of your cabinet.

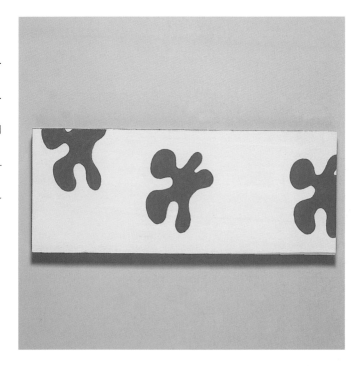

Materials

- Fine sandpaper
- Several large sheets of oak tag or lightweight cardboard
- One can of water-based spray primer
- One can of spray paint, in bright yellow gloss
- Low-tack, double-sided tape
- A roll of painter's masking tape
- One can of spray paint, in bright blue gloss
- One can clear satin spray varnish

- Fine sandpaper
- Tack cloth
- A roll of 1-inch (3 cm) painter's masking tape
- Ruler
- Number-two pencil
- Two paintbrushes: one 2-inch (5 cm) sponge brush for base coat; one ½-inch (1 cm) sponge brush for stripes
- One small can of water-based primer
- One small can of latex-based paint, in pale pink
- One small can of latex-based paint, in medium pink
- One spray can satin-finish polyurethane

PAINTING SURFACE
A small pine bathroom shelf

PATTERN
None required

COMPLETION TIME
Four hours (including drying time)

RATING

Brighten a plain white bathroom with a decorative shelf in warm pink tones. Or choose another soft color to coordinate with your bath linens or a cotton rug. You can adapt the pattern to highlight the silhouette of any simple wooden shelf.

pretty in *pink*

Method

- In this project, the lighter stripes are neatly nestled in the scallop cuts of the bottom portion of the shelf, but you can arrange them any way you like.

- How big should your stripes be? What works for your shelf will depend on how long it is. Rule of thumb: the dark pink stripes should be twice as wide as the pale pink ones. In this case, the pale pink stripes are 1 inch (3 cm) while the dark pink ones are 2 inches (5 cm) wide.

- Make sure you don't cover pencil marks with masking tape as you will most likely not be able to cover them up with the pink paint.

starting *out*

Sand down the shelf and remove any residue with the tack cloth. With the 2-inch (5 cm) brush, paint the shelf with two coats of primer, allowing coats to dry thoroughly in between.

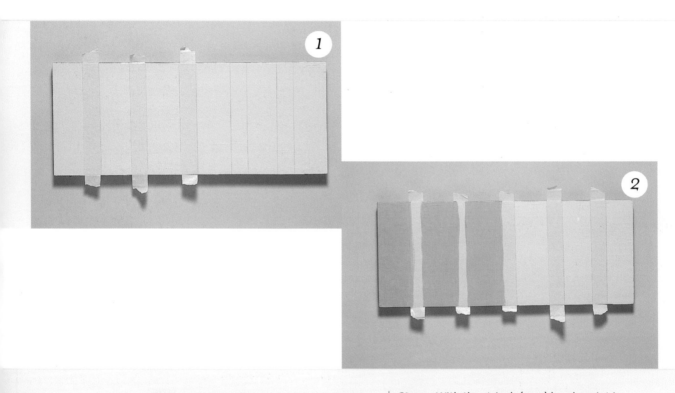

Step 1 Measure the width of the dark pink stripes across the shelf. Mark the width lightly in pencil or with chalk. Mask off the borders of the medium pink stripes.

Step 2 With the ½-inch (1 cm) brush, paint in dark pink stripes, being careful not to cover the masking tape. Carefully remove tape after painting. When the shelf is completely dry, spray with polyurethane top coat and let dry thoroughly.

pink
variation

Starting out with a scalloped shelf? Why not highlight the shape of the piece by accenting the scallops with playful polka dots?

Materials and Method

Use the same basic materials for this project, substituting light spruce green for the base coat and white for the polka dots. You can use the tip of a pencil eraser to create the polka dots. Practice first on a sheet of paper to test out your design. You can also vary the size of the eraser for added interest. To start, prime the shelf and paint two coats of the light spruce green. When the base coat is thoroughly dry, dab the pencil eraser in the white paint and dot the shelf, following the photo to the right.

TIP

If you are not comfortable using a pencil eraser, you can always create a template for the smaller dots, or, depending on the size of your shelf, try using a dime. Larger polka dots can be created using a nickel or quarter.

Blue and white are right at home in a country décor and potted-plant motifs evoke garden images that work just as well in a weekend cottage as they do in an urban space. Distressing the dining set gives it a timeworn casual effect. This project focuses on completing the chair. However, the table legs use the same template as the chair backs.

Materials

- Fine and medium grit sandpaper
- Tack cloth
- Three paintbrushes: one 2-inch (5 cm) sponge brush for base coat, one 1/16-inch (1.5 mm) round liner brush for border, and one 1/8-inch (3 mm) round artist's brush for potted-plant shapes
- One small can of flat-finish latex paint, in blossom white
- One small can of flat-finish latex paint, in deep blue
- Number-two pencil
- Roll of 1-inch (2.5 cm) painter's masking tape
- One spray can satin-finish polyurethane

country *heritage*

TIP

If you are working with a light-toned wood, stain the pieces first in walnut or similarly dark-toned wood stain to make the distressing effect more prominent.

Method

- The potted-plant shapes of this project are large enough that you should be able to paint them in without a problem. However, it never hurts to practice.

- Depending on your skill and confidence level, you may be more comfortable using a stencil. This means that instead of cutting the shapes out and tracing them, you will be using the piece of oak tag you cut the shape out of.

- Paint border in completely freehand, or use masking tape or the edge of the template to paint straight lines for the inside straight border.

PAINTING SURFACE
An unfinished walnut dining set

PATTERN
A potted-plant template and border template (found on pages 122–123)

COMPLETION TIME
Eight hours (including drying time)

RATING //

starting out

Sand down the dining set with fine-grit sandpaper and remove residue with tack cloth. Trace and cut out templates on pages 122–123 and set aside. Do not use primer for this project.

Step 1 With the 2-inch (5 cm) sponge brush, paint the dining set in two coats of the white base coat, allowing the first coat to dry thoroughly before painting the second.

Step 2 Line up border templates on chair back. With number-two pencil, trace templates onto chair.

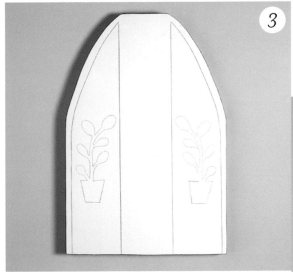

Step 3 Center potted-plant templates within borders, following the photo above. Keeping these in place, trace onto chairback with number-two pencil.

Step 4 With the 1/8-inch (3 mm) round artist's brush and the deep blue paint, carefully paint in the potted-plant templates. Allow to dry thoroughly. With the 1/16-inch (1.5 mm) round liner brush, carefully paint in the borders. If desired, line up masking tape on either side of inner borders and paint within masking tape lines to ensure straight line. Remove the tape immediately after painting. Allow piece to dry overnight.

Step 5 With the sandpaper, gently distress the chair—focusing on the white portions and not the blue. Brush away any residue, spray with polyurethane and let dry.

variation

ritage

Select other typical country shapes to lend a rural elegance to furniture. In this case, red hearts set a distinctly country-casual mood. Other simple typically country shapes you may choose to try out instead are butterflies, daisies and other uncomplicated floral shapes, garden tools, trees, and barns. Find a picture of one of these shapes and trace over it with tracing paper to create your own stencil—or try sketching freehand if you are feeling adventurous.

Materials and Method

Use the same materials for this variation, substituting the heart templates on page 124 for the potted plants and the colonial red paint for the deep blue. You can choose to distress the piece or not, depending on your personal preference. The country feel will come through on its own, with the colors and shapes chosen. Proceed with project following directions on pages 58–60.

Materials

- Medium and fine grit sandpaper
- Tack cloth
- One 2-inch (5 cm) sponge brush for all applications
- One can of water-based primer
- One small can of satin-finish latex paint, in wildflower blue
- One small can of satin-finish latex paint, in colonial red
- Number-two pencil
- Ruler
- A piece of white chalk
- Roll of 2-inch (5 cm) painter's masking tape
- One spray can satin-finish polyurethane

A harlequin pattern is a classic motif that adds style to any décor. The colors chosen for this project lend the piece a decided country flair, but you don't have to be locked into that. Change the feel by using pinks and greens for a traditional harlequin pattern, black and silver for a high-tech mood—whatever colors you choose, the pattern should translate.

classic *motif*

PAINTING SURFACE
A well-weathered pine table

PATTERN
No templates required

COMPLETION TIME
Twelve to fifteen hours (including drying time)

RATING //

Method

- This easy project doesn't require any templates. To complete it, you simply measure lines and paint within the borders.

- Use chalk to draw in lines. It's easy to rub away once the piece is completed and you won't have to worry about covering up pencil lines.

- Start with the blue as your base coat, and paint red over the blue. Typically, it's easier to paint a dark color over a light color rather than the other way around. While in this case, both colors are equally dark, blue is an easier color to paint over than red.

- Try lining up masking tape on the lines before you paint to ensure clean, straight edges.

starting *out*

With fine grit sandpaper sand down the table and remove residue with tack cloth.

Paint the table with two coats of primer.

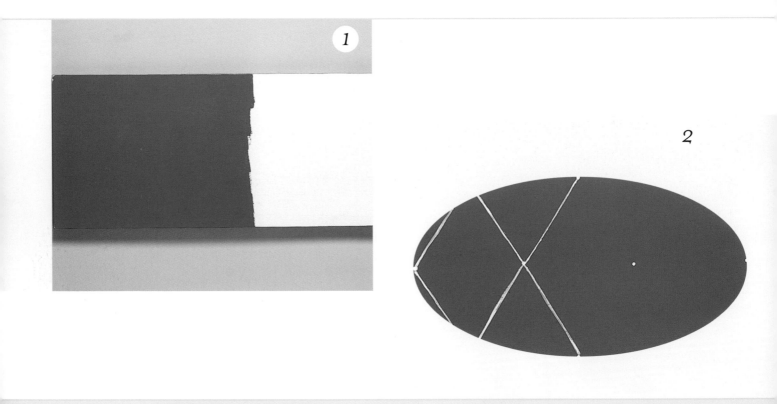

Step 1 With the 2-inch (5 cm) brush, paint the table in two coats of the wildflower blue base coat, allowing the first coat to dry thoroughly before applying the second.

Step 2 With the ruler and chalk, measure and mark placement of diamond shapes on table-top or other surface. Draw in the lines with white chalk.

f

3

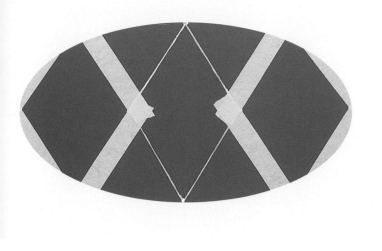

4

Step 3 Line up masking tape on the outside edges of the diamonds that are being painted red. You will only be able to paint the outer two diamonds first. Once they are dry, you can mask off and paint the center diamond.

Step 4 Paint the designated diamonds in colonial red with the 2-inch (5 cm) sponge brush. Carefully peel the tape off before the paint dries to avoid having it dry to the surface. Once the paint has completely dried, repeat the process with the center diamond.

5

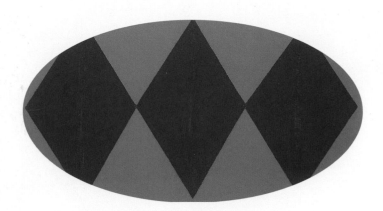

Step 5 Allow the piece to dry overnight. The next morning, distress the table with medium grit sandpaper. For best results, distress only the diamonds, allowing the wildflower blue base coat to shine through.

Step 6 When piece is thoroughly dry, spray with satin-finish polyurethane top coat and let dry.

motif
variation

A checkerboard pattern, with its clean lines and symmetry, is another classic motif. You can do a tight pattern, such as the one we did, or use a larger grid for a cleaner, more open look. Also, we used three different shades of blue, but the effect will be just as strong with just two colors.

Method

Measure the piece to determine how many squares you'll need to allot, and how large they should be. Mark the lines and draw in with a ruler and chalk or pencil. Proceed with project following directions on pages 64–66.

Materials

- Medium and fine sandpaper
- Tack cloth
- One 2-inch (5 cm) sponge brush for all applications
- One can of water-based primer
- One small can of water-based, satin-finish paint in wildflower blue
- One small can of water-based, satin-finish paint in medium blue
- One small can of water-based, satin-finish paint in pale blue
- Number-two pencil
- Ruler
- A piece of white chalk
- Roll of 2-inch (5 cm) painter's masking tape
- One spray can satin-finish polyurethane

Infuse an ordinary entryway with a splash of color—or colorblock. This simple and sunny pattern works well in any contemporary setting. It can be just the piece to highlight other yellow accents in a room, or to add a splash of color to an interior composed mainly of neutrals.

Materials

- Fine sandpaper
- Tack cloth
- A roll of 1-inch (3 cm) painter's masking tape
- Ruler
- Number-two pencil
- Two paintbrushes: one 2-inch (5 cm) sponge brush for base coat; one 1-inch (2.5 cm) sponge brush for stripes
- One small can of water-based primer
- One small can of latex-based paint, in antique white
- One small can of latex-based paint, in medium yellow
- One small can of latex-based paint, in bright yellow
- One spray can satin-finish varnish

colorblock *table*

Method

- This simple project is a great one to start with if you haven't undertaken a painted-furniture project before. The technique requires laying down masking tape and painting with broad strokes.

- Make sure you don't cover pencil marks with masking tape as you will most likely not be able to cover them up with the yellow paint.

- Do not remove all masking tape until you have completed painting in the center color.

PAINTING SURFACE
An unfinished pine table

PATTERN
None required

COMPLETION TIME
Five hours
(including drying time)

RATING

starting out

Sand the table and remove any residue with the tack cloth. With the 2-inch (5 cm) sponge brush, apply the first coat of primer to the table. Let dry thoroughly and apply a second coat. With the 2-inch (5 cm) brush, paint the table completely in the antique white base coat. Let dry thoroughly and apply a second coat.

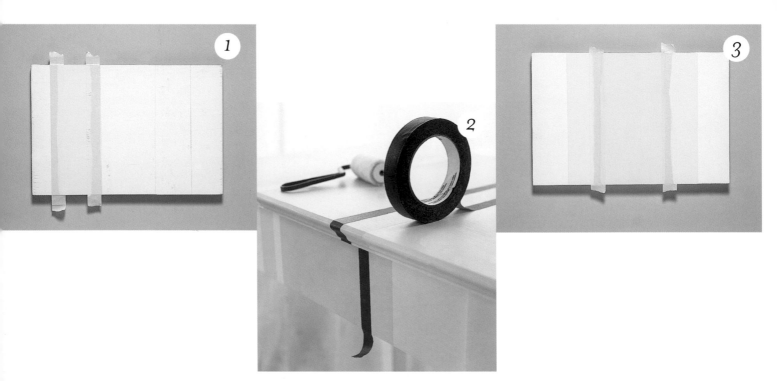

Step 1 With ruler, measure out the boundaries of the three blocks, leaving a 1-inch (3 cm) wide border on each side of the center block. Lightly mark at the top and bottom with number-two pencil. Place 1-inch (3 cm) masking tape along the outside edges of these marks. Paint in the medium yellow blocks with the 1-inch (2.5 cm) sponge brush.

Step 2 Working around the edges of a table can be especially tricky—to keep the stripes even and smooth, ease a low-tack masking tape completely into the grooves of the wood. Then use a detail brush to get a smooth application of paint around these dynamic edges and underneath corners.

Step 3 Once the medium yellow blocks are painted and dry, paint the center block with a 2-inch (5 cm) sponge brush. Remove masking tape immediately once stripes are painted in—this will keep the edge from peeling away, as it does when tape is removed from dry paint. When the table is completely dry, spray with polyurethane top coat and let dry thoroughly.

table variation

Experiment with different color combinations. The black, white, and gray chosen for the variation makes a definitively masculine statement. Blues and greens would look lovely in a lake side cottage or a beach house, or use purple and lavender shades for a teen vanity.

Materials and Method

Use the same materials for the variation, substituting white for the base color, black for the outside blocks, and gray for the center. Also, use ¹/₂-inch (1 cm) painter's masking tape to decrease the width of the outside blocks. Proceed following the directions on page 70.

TIP

Water-based paints are ideal for painted furniture projects because they are easy to apply, dry quickly, and are easily cleaned from brushes and hands. There's a drawback, though. If you are working with a broken-color technique, such as this colorblock table, you may find that the paint dries too quickly, making the masking tape difficult to remove, and hard for mistakes to be wiped away before setting in.

- Fine sandpaper
- Tack cloth
- Four paintbrushes: one 2-inch (5 cm) wide for primer and base coat; one 1/8-inch (3 mm) liner artist's brush for the outside of the paisley shapes; one 1/8-inch (3 mm) flat art brush for the inside of the paisley shapes; one 1/16-inch (1.5 mm) liner brush for border
- One small can of water-based primer
- One small can of flat-finish latex paint in lavender
- One small can of flat-finish latex paint in Violetta
- One small can of flat-finish latex paint in pale lavender
- One small container of acrylic paint in Acra violet
- Ruler
- Number-two pencil
- Roll of 1-inch (2.5 cm) painter's masking tape
- One spray can satin-finish polyurethane

PAINTING SURFACE
A small pine plant table

PATTERN
**Three separate templates
(found on page 125)**

COMPLETION TIME
**Six hours
(including drying time)**

RATING ///

Playful paisley is a welcome addition to any space but is most at home in a spare, minimal décor where the paisley has a chance to shine without competing with other patterns in the room. While this project calls on lavender to accent the playful design, paisley can be fun in any palette. Here, the paisley creates a delightful table-top border for a small plant, simple vase, or objet d'art.

pure *paisley*

TIP

If you are mixing paint to get desired colors, be sure to make extra for touch-ups.

Method

- This project requires a steady hand and very small brushes to properly fill in the tiny shapes. For best results, take a few practice runs before you begin the project.

- Follow the paisley pattern on page 125, or work out one of your own. Trace and cut out several of the paisley shapes and lie them down on the table until you find the arrangement that works for you.

- For larger or smaller shapes, enlarge or reduce the templates with a photocopy machine.

- Paint one color at a time and allow paint to dry thoroughly before proceeding to the next set of shapes.

- Do not overload the brushes or the finish will look blobby.

starting *out*

Sand down the table and remove residue with tack cloth. Paint the table with two coats of primer. With the 2-inch (5 cm) brush, paint the entire table in two coats of lavender, allowing the first coat to dry thoroughly before painting the second. Trace and cut out borders, flourishes, and at least sixteen paisley templates and set aside.

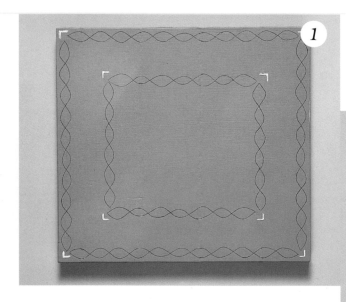

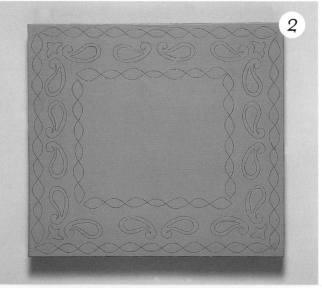

Step 1 With the ruler, measure the location of the outer and inner borders. With chalk, mark the corners of each border. Line up templates on tabletop and trace with number-two pencil.

Step 2 Following photo on page 73, or using your own design, place paisley and flourish templates within borders and trace with number-two pencil.

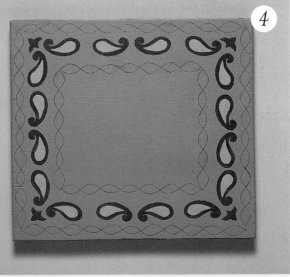

Step 3 With the small liner 1/8-inch (3 mm) brush, paint outside of paisley shapes and flourishes in Violetta. Let dry thoroughly.

Step 4 With the small flat 1/8-inch (3 mm) brush, paint inside of paisley shapes with pale lavender. Let dry thoroughly.

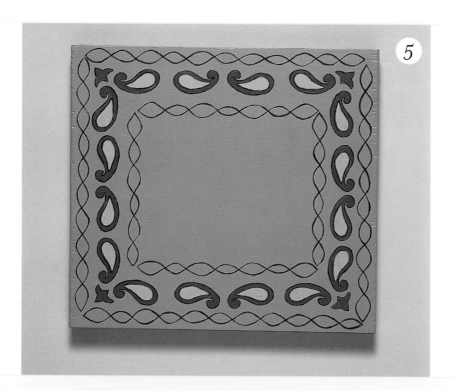

Step 5 With the small round ¹/₁₆-inch (1.5 mm) liner brush, paint the borders with the Acra violet acrylic paint, starting with the inside border. Outline paisley shapes and flourishes with this color. Let dry thoroughly. When piece is thoroughly dry, spray the table with two coats polyurethane and let dry.

variation

This pattern works best with bright, playful colors. You can vary it by changing the colors, the placement of the shapes, or even by using a straight border instead of a squiggly one, as shown below.

Method

Begin following directions on page 74. With the ruler, measure the location of the outside of the outer and inner borders. Outline with number-two pencil. From the outside border, measure in $1/2$ inch and mark location of inside borders with chalk. Outline with number-two pencil. Proceed with project following directions on page 75.

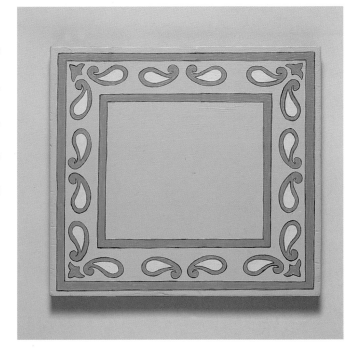

Materials

Use the same materials for this variation, substituting the following greens for the purples:

- One small can of flat-finish latex paint in light spruce for base coat
- One small can of flat-finish latex paint in pale green for inner paisley shapes
- One small container of acrylic paint in bright green/blue for outer paisley shapes and borders

painted *finishes*

This project mimics the look of Caribbean architecture—bright colors painted over plaster and stucco buildings. In this case, spackling putty was used to replicate the texture of stucco. Choose the hot colors of tropical islands to spark a casual contemporary home or, as seen here, to give a traditional home an exotic, tropical look.

Materials

- Extra-fine sandpaper
- Tack cloth to remove dust
- One small container of spackling putty
- One 2-inch (5 cm) -wide putty knife
- One 2-inch (5 cm) -wide paintbrush for tabletop and larger surfaces; one 1-inch (2.5 cm) -wide brush for legs and smaller areas
- One small can of latex-based primer
- One small container of acrylic paint, in hot pink
- One spray can satin-finish polyurethane

caribbean *brights*

TIP

Experiment with putty before you get to the table. On a scrap piece of wood, see what kind of coverage you can get with different amounts. A little can go a long way.

Method

- In this project, apply spackling putty to your furniture piece, and then paint over to mimic the look of Caribbean architecture.

- Don't be discouraged if you can't wield a putty knife like a pro.

- Once dried, and before you move on to the primer stage, you can sand down the putty to make it look less globby.

- Don't worry if you have to prime the piece before you can gauge if the texture is right. You can sand it down after the primer stage—just be sure to paint another coat of primer once you're through.

- There's no rule about how much texture you should add to your table. This project shows a very light treatment, but you can add more texture if that appeals to you.

PAINTING SURFACE
A demi-lune wood table, stripped of paint and varnishes.

PATTERN
None required

COMPLETION TIME
Seven to ten hours (including drying time)

RATING ////

starting *out*

Sand down the entire table and then wipe with a tack cloth to remove residue.

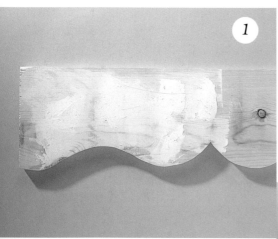

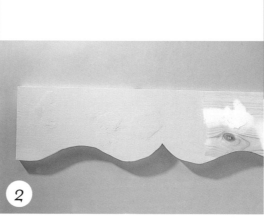

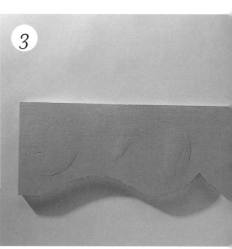

Step 1 With putty knife, scoop a dollop of putty and apply it to the wood in uneven swatches and not too thick. Smooth down with the edge of the knife to thin the putty. Once you have an acceptable thickness, allow to dry for at least one to two hours, depending on thickness of putty layer. Once dry, sand down any parts that look too bumpy.

Step 2 Apply a coat of primer over the plaster with the 2-inch (5 cm) brush. Paint with the grain of the wood. Allow first coat to dry for at least two hours. If needed, apply a second coat and allow to dry for an additional two hours.

Step 3 Paint over the primer coat with the hot pink paint, painting with the grain. Use the 2-inch (5 cm) brush for the large surfaces (in this case, the table top and apron), and the 1-inch (2.5 cm) brush for smaller, hard-to-reach areas. Let dry for one hour. Apply a second coat, if needed, and let dry for one hour.

Step 4 Apply polyurethane finish. Two coats are recommended.

v a r i a t i o n

Another feature of Caribbean architecture is sun-faded color. With a little practice, you can create this illusion. The trick is to remove the finish color with medium sandpaper. The white base coat peeks through the color giving the piece a weathered look without detracting from the dazzle of the pink.

Method

For this project, sand down and remove residue from the table, but skip the plastering phase altogether. With the 2-inch (5 cm) brush, apply a coat of primer. Let dry for two hours, and apply a second coat. Also with the 2-inch (5 cm) brush, apply two coats of the white base coat, allowing it to dry for about two hours, between applications. With the 2-inch (5 cm) brush, apply two coats of the hot pink paint to the larger surfaces (in this case, the table top and apron), and use the 1-inch (2.5 cm) brush for smaller, hard-to-reach areas. Let the second coat dry overnight. The next day, take the sandpaper and rub away at selected areas of the table, using the picture on page 80 as your guide.

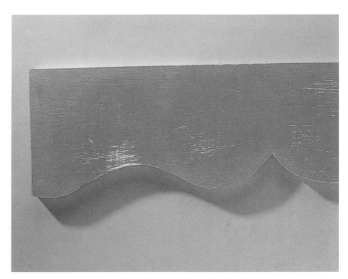

TIP

Work with the form of your table to create degrees of fading that look realistic. That is, the part most exposed to the sun would show more white than other parts.

Materials

Have most of the same materials on hand for the variation, except for the putty and putty knife. Include the following:
- One small can of latex base coat, in bright white
- One sheet of medium sandpaper (100 grit)

- Fine sandpaper
- Tack cloth
- A small, thick, 100 percent cotton towel
- A 6-ounce bag of milk paint powder, in federal blue
- 6 ounces of water in a 16-ounce, or larger, container to mix the milk paint powder
- One small can clear satin varnish, specifically manufactured to cover a milk paint finish
- One 2-inch (5 cm) sponge brush, for applying varnish
- One small can of acrylic paint, in federal blue, for knobs (optional)

Give your living room or bedroom a dose of Shaker simplicity—and color—by painting a plain armoire with this Shaker rub technique. The color and texture of the wood you use will have a big effect on the piece as the paint is not meant to cover the whole surface area of the piece, so the wood you choose will peek through.

shaker rubbed

PAINTING SURFACE
An unfinished cedar cabinet

PATTERN
None required

COMPLETION TIME
Three hours (including drying time)

RATING

TIP

Milk paint does not adhere to metal, glass, or ceramic knobs. Your options: replace your ceramic knobs with wood knobs, keep your knobs and paint in acrylic to match, or simply leave knobs unpainted.

Method

- Sand the piece, mix the paint, rub the paint over the piece, let dry. A rub is one of the easiest ways to create a dramatic effect on an ordinary piece of furniture.

- To save time, you can keep the cabinet doors on.

- Depending on the materials your hardware and knobs are made from, you may have to paint these in acrylic, and milk paint will not adhere to most metals.

- Keep in mind that with milk paint, a little goes a long way. When doing a rub technique, you don't want to completely cover your wood, so don't glob the paint onto your rag. If you apply the paint too thickly, you will mask the grain of the wood and ruin the effect of the rub.

starting *out*

Remove all knobs from an unfinished or stripped cabinet. Be sure your piece is unfinished or stripped because this tech-nique is just not effective otherwise, as seen below. Also, do not use primer. You do not have to remove cabinet doors to perform this technique, but if you are more comfortable working this way, go ahead and remove the doors. Sand down the cabinet doors and frame and wipe with tack cloth to remove residue.

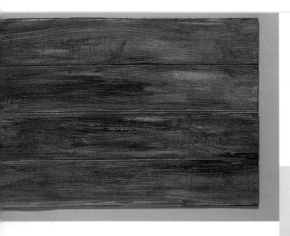

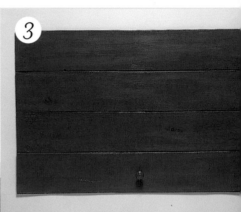

Painting over a finished or primed piece will not give you the desired effect, as seen above.

Step 1 Mix the milk paint powder with the base, following manufacturer's directions. Milk paint uses equal proportions of milk paint powder to water, so measure accordingly.

Step 2 Ball the cotton towel up in your hand, keeping the ends in the palm of your hand and the middle part out. Dip this middle part of the towel into the paint mixture, making sure you get an even application. Do not soak the rag in the milk paint mixture. Lightly and care-fully, rub the paint into the wood in a circular motion or with the grain of the wood. It does-n't matter which of these methods you use, just be consistent.

Note: Do not apply a second coat of the milk paint, which may lead to an undesired opaque finish.

Step 3 Apply one coat of the special varnish to cabinet with a sponge brush. Allow to dry for two hours, then apply a second coat. Allow second coat to dry overnight.

rubbed variation

If you want the look of a Shaker rub, but you don't want to introduce bright colors into your décor, use a shade of paint that echoes the look of natural wood, such as barn red, which will make the piece look less painted and more like a richer wood.

Method

Follow the directions for the original project, this time using the barn red paint. Apply the paint lightly in this case to let the grain of the cedar really shine through.

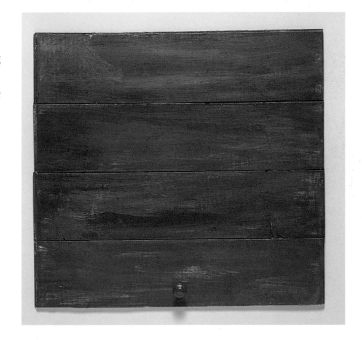

TIP

You can control the degree of coverage by adding more water to the paint. The more water you add to milk paint, the thinner the paint will be and, thus, the less opaque the finish. In this case, you should thin out the paint so that the application will be more of a stain than a coating.

Materials

Same as for original project, but this time:
- A 6-ounce bag of milk paint powder, in barn red
- At least 6 ounces of water in a 16-ounce, or larger, container in which you will mix the milk paint powder
- One small can of acrylic paint, in barn red, for knobs (optional)

Create a feeling of Provence with a simple painting technique. This gray distressed cabinet captures the tenets of French country style—elegant but not fussy, upscale yet warm and homey. The distressed finish gives it just the right dose of cozy, country charm. This fairly simple method involves painting a cabinet, drying, and scratching off the paint with sandpaper to achieve a timeworn look.

french country

Method

- If the piece has glass doors, be sure to cover the perimeter of the glass panes with painter's masking tape. Do not paint completely over the tape or it will be difficult to remove.

- If you have a light wood piece but like the effect of dark wood peeking through, stain the piece in American Walnut or similar dark wood stain before you begin.

- The dryer the paint, the easier it will be to scrape off. If possible, allow the piece to dry overnight before distressing.

- The more you sand, the more distressed the cabinet, so do a little at a time. Use the photo on the opposite page as a guide.

Materials

- Several sheets of medium sandpaper
- Tack cloth for removing residue
- 2-inch (5 cm) masking tape to mask off glass doors
- One small can of water-based wood stain, in American Walnut (optional)
- A synthetic bristle brush for applying stain (optional)
- Soft cotton rag for wiping off excess stain (optional)
- One 2-inch (5 cm) synthetic bristle brush or 2-inch (5 cm) sponge brush
- One small can of flat, interior latex paint, in light gray
- Enough craft paper or newspaper to cover glass panes
- One spray can satin-finish polyurethane

PAINTING SURFACE
A stripped, walnut wood china cabinet

PATTERN
None required

COMPLETION TIME
**Six hours
(including drying time)**

RATING

starting *out*

Prep the cabinet for painting by removing handles or drawer pulls and lining windowpanes with masking tape so paint won't get on the glass. Sand down the cabinet and remove residue with tack cloth.

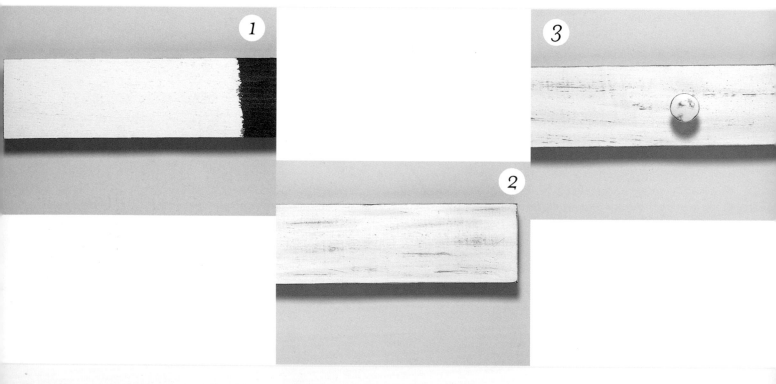

Step 1 Stain the cabinet in American Walnut, if necessary, following manufacturer's directions. Let dry. Paint two coats of gray over the entire cabinet, painting with the grain of the wood, and allow to dry completely.

Step 2 With medium-grit sandpaper, and using the picture on page 88 as a guide, sand away at the gray paint, revealing streaks of the wood underneath.

Step 3 Remove residue with tack cloth. Cover glass with kraft or newspaper and tape down. Spray the finished piece with protective top coat. Remove masking tape and paper from glass. Allow piece to dry overnight. Replace hardware.

country variation

Distressing is one way to give a piece an aged look, but it's not the only way. Applying a crackle finish achieves a similar effect. To add an antique patina to a crackle finish, rub a tinted furniture wax over the surface—it will darken the space between the cracks.

Method

With brush, apply the base coat and allow to dry for several hours or overnight. Paint over base coat with crackling medium.

Let crackling medium dry thoroughly (about two hours). Then apply the top coat. Don't be discouraged if crackling doesn't show up immediately. As top coat dries, the crackling effect begins to appear.

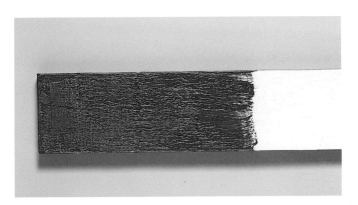

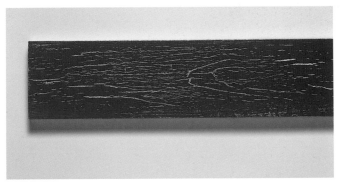

TIP

Crackling medium is a water-based medium and works very well with water-based paints and glazes. Never use an oil-based paint with crackle medium, as the oil and water will not mix properly and your results will be disappointing— to say the least.

Materials

Same as for original project, but substitute:
- One small can of flat, interior latex paint, in white
- One small can of crackling medium
- A 1 1/2-inch (4 cm) disposable synthetic-bristle brush
- One small can of flat-finish latex paint, in dark blue

- Several sheets of medium sandpaper
- Tack cloth for removing residue
- 2-inch (5 cm) masking tape to mask off glass doors
- One thick, 100 percent cotton rag
- One small can of flat, interior latex paint, in bright red
- Enough kraft paper or newspaper to cover glass panes
- One spray can satin-finish polyurethane

Transform a kitchen or dining room into an English country house with this charming piece. English cottages are often steeped in tradition, with families passing down the homes—and the items within those homes—through the generations. A hutch is a great place to showcase these items, both old and new. This project is actually two in one: it involves both a rub technique (as done in the Shaker Rubbed on pages 84–87) and a distressing technique, as in the French Country distressed cabinet on pages 89–91. The effect is timeless piece that looks several generations old.

english *cottage*

PAINTING SURFACE
A simple beech wood hutch

PATTERN
None required

COMPLETION TIME
Six hours
(including drying time)

RATING //

Method

- If the piece has glass doors, be sure to cover the perimeter of the glass panes with painter's masking tape. Do not paint completely over the tape or it will be difficult to remove.

- The dryer the paint, the easier it will be to sand off. If possible, allow the piece to dry overnight before distressing.

- The more you sand, the more distressed the cabinet, so do a little at a time. Use the photo on page 93 as a guide.

- This project works best on light wood such as pine or white fir. Using a darker wood will produce a very different effect.

starting *out*

Prep the cabinet for painting by removing handles or drawer pulls and lining glass with masking tape so paint won't get on the glass. Sand down the cabinet and remove residue with tack cloth. Do not apply a primer coat.

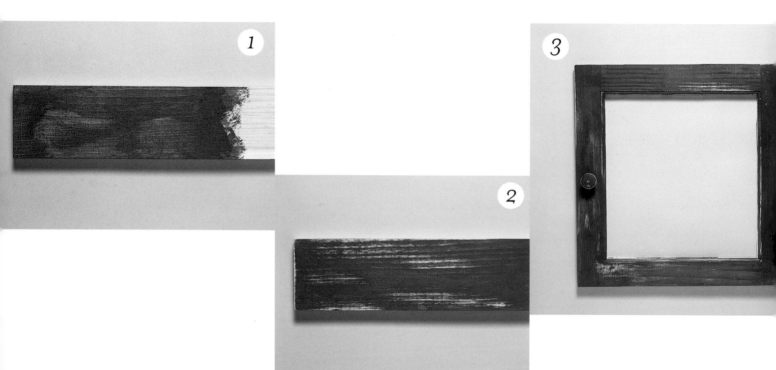

Step 1 With the cotton rag, rub the bright red paint into the cabinet, using an up-and-down with the grain or circular technique. Let the cabinet dry overnight.

Step 2 With the sandpaper, sand away at the rubbed-on paint in parts to reveal the wood underneath.

Step 3 Remove residue with the tack cloth. Cover glass with kraft or newspaper and tape down. Spray the finished piece with protective top coat. Remove masking tape and paper from glass. Allow piece to dry overnight. Replace hardware.

cottage
variation

The gist of this look is well-worn paint that imbues a piece of furniture with a cozy country charm. Get a similar look by applying the paint with a sponge treatment.

Method

Proceed as in the original project, except instead of applying paint with a rag, apply with the sponge. Load the sponge sparingly with paint, dab it on the wood surface varying the amount of pressure of the application to give it a multitoned look. Overloading the sponge will result in a blotchy finish and the sponging effect will not be visible. Vary the paint application by changing pressure of sponge against wood surface.

TIP

With this technique, you will only need to sand the piece before you paint it; however, if you want to create a distressed look, sand off the sponged-on paint once it's had a chance to dry overnight.

Materials

Use same as for original project, but this time apply with a painter's natural wool sea sponge

Dining al fresco in a sunny courtyard is one of the great pleasures of the Mediterranean experience. Another is the beauty of the furniture on which dining is enjoyed. In this case, a lacquer technique, with its rich colors and sleek texture, brightens up an outdoor dining "room." Use this technique to brighten up your own kitchen or dining area—or try it in other areas of the home.

Materials

- Several sheets of extra-fine sandpaper
- Tack cloth for removing residue
- 2-inch (5 cm) sponge brush
- One small can of water-based primer, tinted to match paint (for intense colors only)
- One small can of semigloss interior latex paint, in bright blue
- One spray can gloss-finish polyurethane

mediterranean *lacquer*

Method

- Sanding is the most important step in creating a smooth lacquer finish. This project involves numerous sanding phases so be sure to have plenty of sandpaper.

- Consider investing in a palm sander. Black & Decker makes a model called the Mouse, which is lightweight, handheld, and easy to use.

- The other secret of flawless lacquer is using a deep, rich color of paint for permanence. The idea is to create a very deep, rich, and slick surface. A high-gloss top coat provides the much-desired shine.

- To get the best results, do not use a bristle brush, which will make more work by creating subtle grooves in the paint that will ultimately need to be sanded down.

PAINTING SURFACE
A stripped maple table

PATTERN
None required

COMPLETION TIME
**Eighteen hours
(including drying time)**

RATING ///

starting *out*

Thoroughly sand down the table several times and remove residue with tack cloth. Look at the piece closely in a well-lit place and run your hand over every surface to make sure there are no little bumps. You will not get a perfect, smooth, lacquered finish if you are not meticulous at sanding (see below).

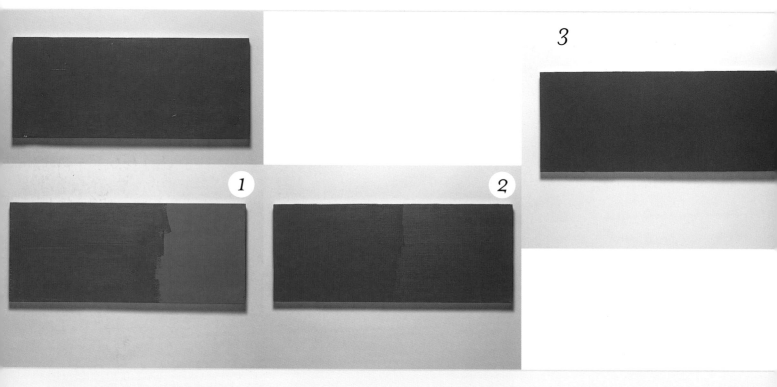

Step 1 Apply the first coat of primer and let dry overnight. Sand, wipe down with tack cloth, and apply second coat of primer. Let dry, then sand and wipe down with tack cloth. Paint over the primer coat. Let dry, then sand again. Wipe away residue with tack cloth.

Step 2 Repaint surface. You will notice that the second coat makes the color on the surface darker and richer in tone. Let dry thoroughly. Run your hand across the surface, making sure there are no bumps.

Step 3 Cover the piece with two coats of polyurethane.

lacquer
variation

The most common colors for lacquer are black and white, but that does-n't mean you have to be confined to these. Mediterranean style comes alive with bright colors. This variation uses orange to mimic the terra-cotta tone so popular in Mediterranean design.

Method

Thoroughly sand down surface several times, removing residues between each sanding with tack cloth. Run your hand over every inch of the surface to make sure there are no bumps. The bright orange shade used for this variation will be less for-giving in revealing surface flaws than the dark blue. Proceed following the directions on page 98.

TIP

For best results, use an electric hand sander for this project. It will give you more even coverage and save you a lot of extra work.

Materials

- Several sheets of extra-fine sandpaper
- Tack cloth
- 2-inch (5 cm) sponge brush
- One small can of water-based primer, tinted to match paint
- One small can of semi-gloss, inte-rior latex paint, in bright orange
- One spray can gloss-finish polyurethane

Materials

- Several sheets of fine sandpaper
- Tack cloth for removing residue
- 2-inch (5 cm) sponge brush or 1 1/2 inch (4 cm) brush for base coat; 1 1/2 inch (4 cm) brush for paint and clear glaze coats
- One small can of water-based primer
- One small can of bright white water-based paint for base coat
- One small can of light gray paint for top coat
- One small can of water-based glaze
- One spray can satin-finish polyurethane

PAINTING SURFACE
A built-in pine cabinet

PATTERN
None required

COMPLETION TIME
Six hours
(including drying time)

RATING //

A colorwash treatment can be used in almost any décor but looks best within casual, simple, design schemes. Consider continuing the technique throughout the rest of the room, as was done here, or let the piece stand on its own.

timeless *colorwash*

Method

- A colorwash technique is simply a blending of a color with a glaze to create an uneven, almost swirled effect with the chosen color. So while a sponge or rag may also be used in this technique, a bristle brush creates the best contrast, necessary when washing with a light color. The method also creates a sheer look—the paint mixed with glaze reveals some of the base coat beneath (in this case, a white base coat).

- Colorwash can be applied in many different ways—in a circular motion, against the grain of the wood—but the most effective method for this particular project is with the grain of the wood.

- The base coat in a colorwash need not always be white. Try mixing and matching complementary colors.

- For a more subtle effect, add more glaze to the paint mixture.

starting *out*

Prep the cabinet for painting by removing handles or drawer pulls and lining windowpanes with masking tape so paint won't get on the glass. Sand down the cabinet and remove residue with tack cloth. Prime piece with one coat of water–based primer.

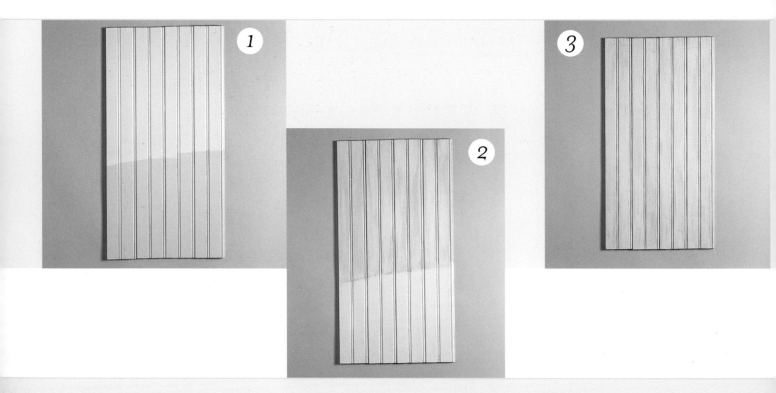

Step 1 Using 2-inch (5 cm) sponge brush or 1 1/2 inch (4 cm) bristle brush, apply two coats of the base coat to cabinet and allow to dry.

Step 2 Mix one part of the light gray paint with five parts glaze. Apply to cabinet in the direction of the wood grain, which is the same direction as the vertical grooves in the wood.

Step 3 Allow the glaze and paint mixture to dry on the cabinet overnight. Then, spray the finished piece with two coats of polyurethane.

variation

The colorwash technique can be very subtle, as shown in the original project, or it can be bold and unmistakable. The more dominant the color, the more contrast in the colorwash project. Vary the statement you make with a colorwash treatment by using a brighter, bolder color—in this case, bright green.

Method

Sand down the piece of furniture you will be painting and remove residue with a tack cloth. Prime the piece with a water-based primer and paint over with white base coat. If you decide instead to use an oil-based primer and base coat, be sure to also use an oil-based glaze. Mix one part of the bright green paint with five parts glaze. Proceed following the directions on page 102.

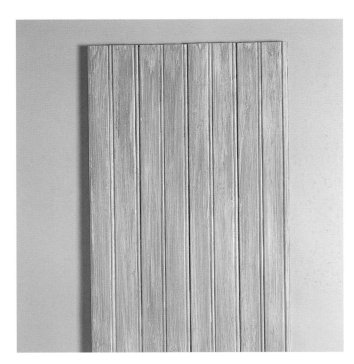

TIP

Glazes dry very quickly, so it is important to work quickly when applying a glaze. While you want contrast in your colorwash project, you don't want it to look uneven. Be sure to practice your technique before starting your furniture piece. Also, check your paint store for an extender product to lengthen the drying time of the glaze.

Materials

- Several sheets of fine sandpaper
- Tack cloth
- 2-inch (5 cm) sponge brush or 1 1/2-inch (4 cm) for base coat; 1 1/2-inch (4 cm) brush for paint and clear glaze coats
- One small can of water-based primer
- One small can of bright white water-based paint for basecoat
- One small can of light green paint for topcoat
- One small can of water-based glaze
- One spray can satin-finish polyurethane

This pickled bureau is most at home in a country décor, but depending on the color of paint or stain you choose, it can be adapted to just about any design scheme. Pickling is a simple technique that involves watering down paint, covering a surface, then wiping the excess off that surface so that the natural grain of the wood shows through the color or stain. In this project, the pickling method on light pine creates an almost powdery effect.

- Several sheets of fine sandpaper
- Tack cloth for removing residue
- 2-inch (5 cm) sponge brush
- One small can of flat-finish latex paint, in light blue
- One quart of water
- One thick, 100 percent cotton rag
- One spray can satin-finish polyurethane

traditional *pickled*

TIP

Be sure to blot the rag you are working with several times in the process of wiping off excess paint on your furniture piece. This will ensure a more even finish.

Method

- Do not let the paint dry on the wood before wiping it away. Also, be sure to wipe off most of the paint just a few minutes after applying so it has time to soak into the wood slightly.

- Pine is very porous, which makes it an ideal material for this technique. However, other porous woods will be just as effective.

- Don't stop with your furniture if you like the way this technique turns out. Pickling is a wonderful finish for hardwood floors, kitchen cabinets, and wood-paneled walls. It will lend a delightful touch of country living to any room.

PAINTING SURFACE
A pine bureau

PATTERN
None required

COMPLETION TIME
Four hours
(including drying time)

RATING

starting *out*

Remove drawers from dresser and remove handles or knobs from drawer fronts. Sand down the dresser and drawers and remove residue with tack cloth. Do not use a primer for this project.

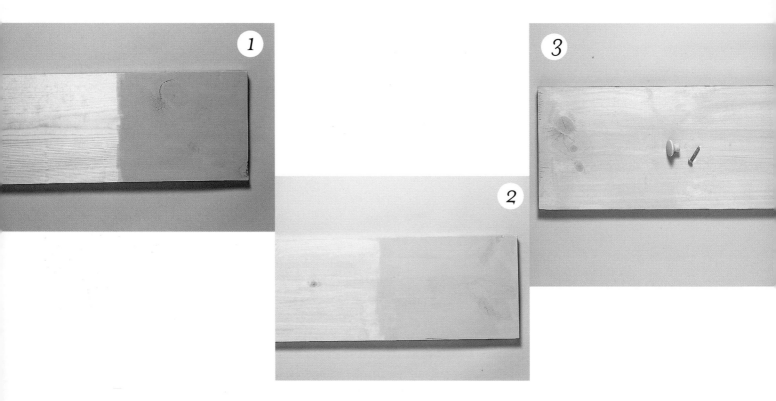

Step 1 Mix the paint with the water, 1 part paint to 3 parts water. With the 2-inch (5 cm) sponge brush, paint the watered-down mixture over the drawers and the dresser frame.

Step 2 With the cotton rag, wipe excess paint off the painted piece. You will notice how the water has allowed the paint to have a sheer quality and be easily wiped off to show the wood grain below.

Step 3 Replace handles or knobs and apply two coats of polyurethane, allowing top coat to dry for at least one hour between applications. The knobs, if also made of wood, can be painted with the same method to match the drawers.

variation

For a more traditional pickling effect, use a wood stain instead of paint. That way, you can enjoy the way this technique comes out in even the most formal room, where colored furniture won't necessarily fly.

Method

Choose a wood stain that matches other furniture pieces in the room where the piece will go—or try something very different to make the piece really stand out. Sand down your furniture piece and wipe residue clean with tack cloth. Do not use a primer for this project. Mix stain with water, one part stain to three parts water. Proceed following the directions on page 106.

TIP

Sometimes seeing the knots of a wood like pine through a finish lends an air of charm to the piece. But if you are a stickler for a smooth and even finish, and you are working with a knotty piece of wood, this might not be the right technique for you. Instead, try a Shaker rub, where you'll be better able to control what the paint covers while still ending up with a countrified piece.

Materials

- Several sheets of fine sandpaper
- Tack cloth
- 2-inch (5 cm) sponge brush
- One small can of water-based wood stain
- One quart of water
- One thick, 100 percent cotton rag
- One spray can satin-finish polyurethane

- Several sheets of extra-fine sandpaper
- Tack cloth for removing residue
- One small can of wood stain, in American Walnut (optional)
- A 2-inch (5 cm) synthetic-bristle brush to apply stain (optional)
- A soft cotton rag for wiping off excess stain (optional)
- One small can of furniture wax
- A soft cotton rag for applying furniture wax
- 1 ½ inch (4 cm) bristle brush
- One small can of flat-finish latex paint, in dark blue
- One small can of flat-finish latex paint, in light blue
- Putty knife
- One spray can satin-finish polyurethane

PAINTING SURFACE
A stripped walnut dresser

PATTERN
None required

COMPLETION TIME
**Six hours
(including drying time)**

RATING ///

Typical Italian country homes were once the homes of farmhands that had been in the same families for generations, but were all but abandoned in the mid–twentieth century for the lure of big cities. Later revisited, these homes were lovingly restored, leaving the charm of generations of country living. The aging technique makes a furniture piece look as though many years—and many more layers of paint—have gone into making the piece look just right. In this project, furniture wax and different shades of the same paint are used to create the illusion of generations of wear and tear.

italian country *bureau*

Method

- If you have a light-wood cabinet but you like the effect of dark wood peeking through, stain the cabinet first in American Walnut or similar stain.

- Keep a sketch of where you've applied the furniture wax so you know exactly where to scrape away at it.

- Do not allow the paint to dry thoroughly as it will be too difficult to remove.

starting *out*

Remove the drawers from dresser. Remove handles or knobs from the drawers. Sand down the dresser and drawers and remove residue with tack cloth. Do not use a primer for this project. If you are working with a light-wood dresser, stain the piece first with dark, water-based stain, following manufacturer's directions.

Step 1 With soft cotton rag, apply furniture wax to the areas where you want the color of the wood to show through. Here, it has been applied along the edges of the drawer front. Using the 1 1/2-inch (4 cm) bristle brush, paint the light blue paint over the furniture wax, painting with the grain of the wood.

Step 2 While the first coat is still wet, apply the deep blue paint, blending it into the lighter shade. Let dry for at least forty minutes to one hour, but no longer.

Step 3 With putty knife, scrape off the areas of paint applied over the furniture wax. Then, with the sandpaper, smooth over any rough areas created by the putty knife.

variation

Try a terra-cotta tone for a classic Italian country effect.

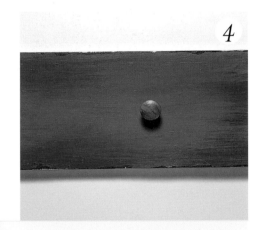

Step 4 Spray the finished piece with two coats of polyurethane. When thoroughly dry, replace all hardware and knobs.

Materials and Method

Use the same materials as for the original project, this time substituting one small can of light orange paint and one small can of dark orange paint for the light and dark blues. Proceed following the directions on pages 110–111.

templates

This section contains templates and stencils for many of the projects in the patterns section of the book. The size of the piece of furniture you will be painting will determine how large—or small—the templates should be. Enlarge or reduce pages on a photocopy machine to get the desired template size for your furniture project.

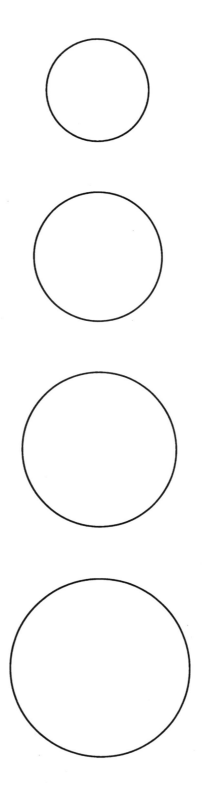

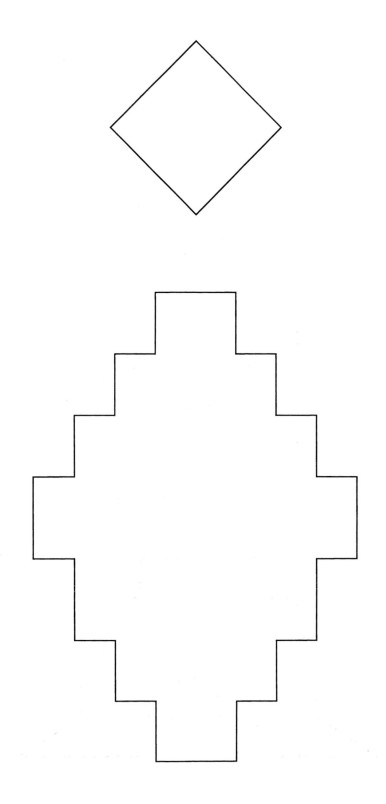

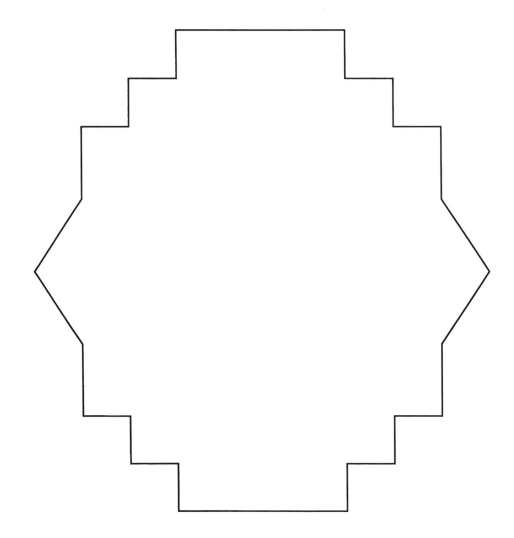

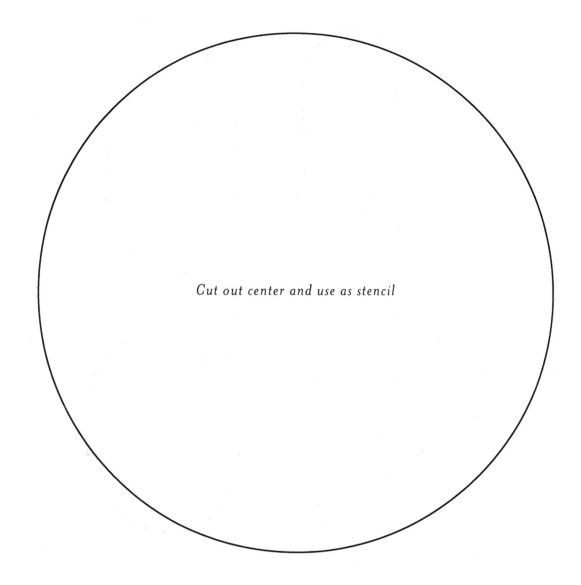

Cut out center and use as stencil

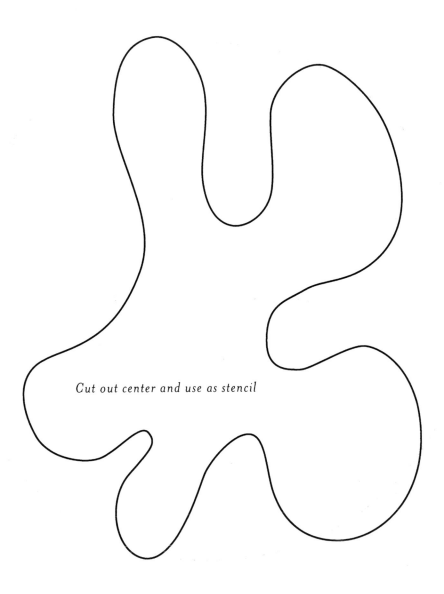

Cut out center and use as stencil

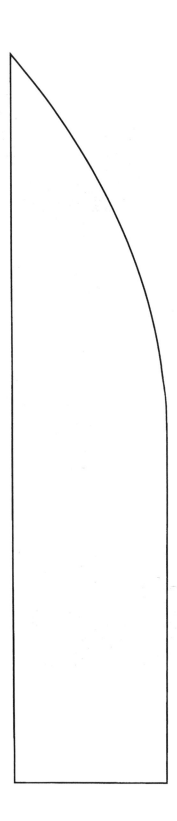

Resources

PAINT

Behr Process Corporation
3400 West Segerstrom Avenue
Santa Ana, CA 92704
1-800-854-0133
www.behrpaint.com

Benjamin Moore
51 Chestnut Ridge Road
Montvale, NJ 07645
1-800-344-0400
www.benjaminmoore.com
bm@att.net

Glidden
925 Enclid Avenue
Cleveland, OH 44115
1-800-221-4100
www.gliddenpaints.com

Martha Stewart Paint
Martha By Mail
11316 North 46th Street
Tampa, FL 33617
1-800-950-7130
www.marthabymail.com
marthabymail@customersvc.com

The Home Depot
Consumer Affairs
2455 Paces Ferry Road
Atlanta, GA 30339
(770) 433-8211
www.homedepot.com

Janovic
30-35 Thomson Avenue
Long Island City, NY 11101
1-800-772-4381
fax (718) 784-4564
www.janovic.com

Pratt and Lambert
1-800-BUYPRAT
www.prattandlambert.com

The Sherwin-Williams Company
www.sherwin.com

ART SUPPLIES

Discount Art Supplies
PO Box 1169
Conway, NH 03818
1-800-547-3264
fax (603) 447-3488
www.discountart.com

Michaels Stores Inc.
8000 Bent Branch
Irving, TX 75063
1-800-MICHAELS
www.michaels.com

Pearl Paint
308 Canal Street
New York, NY 10013
1-800-221-6845
www.pearlpaint.com

StenSource International, Inc.
18971 Hess Avenue
Sonora, CA 95370
1-800-642-9293
fax (209) 536-1805
www.stensource.com
*Online catalog for painting stencils

Liberty Design Company
Portsmouth Avenue
Stratham, NH 03885
www.libertydesign.com
*Stenciling supplies, paint, brushes

Stencil Craft
www.freespace.virgin.net/stencil.craft
stencil.craft@virgin.net
*Original stencil designs, supplies

FURNITURE

A Big Warehouse
635 West Commerce Street
Gilbert, AZ 85234
1-800-249-4941
www.abigwarehouse.com
info@abigwarehouse.com

Bare Furniture
1680 Riverdale Street
West Springfield, MA 01089
(413) 781-0333
fax (413) 737-2342
www.barefurnitureandreproductions.com
barefurniture@yahoo.com

Furniture Gallery
1135 Highway One
Lewes, DE 19958
1-888-808-6104
www.furnituregalleryinc.com
furnituregal@ce.net

Crate & Barrel
1860 West Jefferson Avenue
Naperville, IL 60540
1-800-967-6696
www.crateandbarrel.com

Country Woods Unfinished Furniture
Outlet
Route 27 (Business Route 101)
Raymond, NH 03077
(603) 895-4118
www.countrywoodsunfinished.com
*Furniture, finishing tips

IKEA
Ikea Catalog Department
185 Discovery Drive
Colmar, PA 18915
1-800-434-IKEA
www.ikea-usa.com

Pop's Unfinished Furniture
8911 Reseda Boulevard
Northridge, CA 91324
1-888-838-0707
(818) 717-0707
www.popsfurniture.com
popsfurniture@yahoo.com

Solid Woods, Inc.
40 West Jubal Early Drive
Winchester, VA 22601
(540) 662-0647
fax (540) 662-0672
www.swuf.com
info@swuf.com

Unpainted Furniture City
135 North Broadway
Hicksville, NY 11801
(516) 433-5424

PHOTO CREDITS

The Glidden Company, 13; 41; 44; 53;
    55; 68
Eric Roth, 56; 79 (right)
Picture Press: Schner Wohnen,
    Photographer: Thurmann, 4
Picture Press: Deco, Photographer:
    Thurmann, 78 (left); 88; 101; 104
Picture Press: Deco, Photographer:
    Heye, 79 (left); 80; 96
Picture Press: Deco, Photographer:
    Nüttgens, 78 (right); 85; 92; 108
Report-Bilder-Dienst: Freundin,
    Manduzio, 20 (left), 34
Report-Bilder-Dienst: ©U2
    Fotodesign, 21 (left), 22, 29
Report-Bilder-Dienst: Freundin,
    Spachmann, 21 (right); 46
All studio photography
    by Kevin Thomas

Acknowledgments

Many more people are in on the book-creating process than the names that appear on the jacket. If not for the following people, we never could have accomplished what we did. We are truly thankful for their efforts.

Shawna Mullen believed in our talents as a team and signed us up to do this project. Mary Ann Hall took over the editorial and gave the book a wonderful vision. Ralph Bankes shepherded the project, making sure nothing fell through the cracks. Ron Hampton sweated all the details. Jay Donahue and Kristy Mulkern were patient and kind when it came to deadlines. Silke Braun found beautiful photos for us to step out, and Leeann Leftwich's design helped bring the projects to life.

And we certainly can't leave out our family and friends who gave us their love and support throughout the project. Deepest thanks to the Hornbergers, the Pattersons, the Pardalis family, Randi Gordon, Nellie Patterson, and J.L. Rollings for their enthusiasm. Special thanks goes to Christine Guarino Mayer, who compiled the resource list in the back of the book. Last but not least, thank you to Carl Arnheiter, the grumpiest messenger boy this side of the Hudson River. Without him, we might never have met each other—let alone put a book together.

About the Authors

Virginia Patterson is a fine arts–trained painter. For more than ten years, she has been commissioned to paint everything from traditional canvases to decorative indoor and outdoor murals to unusual objects such as mailboxes, flower boxes, glass pieces, and more. Ms. Patterson regularly restores furniture for interior designers, including staining and upholstery, and has also designed and painted furniture pieces in her original designs. Additionally, Virginia is an accomplished quilter whose work has been exhibited in galleries and art shows across the United States.

Francine Hornberger edits interior design and crafts books. She's written for craft product manufacturers and craft book publishers, including the Offray Ribbon Company and McCall's Creates.